Awakening Your Life Skills

Awakening Your Life Skills

*A light-hearted, pragmatic
and humorous approach to
leading a less stressful life*

SUSAN STERN

CAPRICORN PRESS
Toronto

Canadian Cataloguing in Publication Data

Susan Stern 1942-
Awakening your life skills: a light-hearted, pragmatic & humorous approach to leading a less stressful life

ISBN 0-9685571-0-4

1. Simplicity. 2. Lifestyles. 3. Self-help techniques. I. Title.

BF637.C5S715 1999   646.7   C99-931959-0

Designed by Fortunato Design Inc.
Printed in Canada by Transcontinental Printing

Distributed by:
Hushion House Publishing Limited
36 Northline Road, Toronto, Ontario
M4B 3E2

CAPRICORN PRESS
Suite 103 - 232 Heath Street West
Toronto, Ontario M5P 1N8

"Susan's experiences has led her to a life of educating people toward their own wisdom, rather that duplicating anyone else's. Her advice is practical, funny and important for anyone interested in "learning the ropes" in a wide range of situations It's not for nothing that the Hungarians invented goulash - lots of meat, vegetables and plenty of paprika! Enjoy!"

RABBI LARRY PINSKER
Congregation Darchei Noam

"The more people inform themselves about their own wellness, the healthier our society will be. This book is full of practical wisdom which guides and encourages us to take responsibility for staying well."

DR.CAROLYN BENNETT
Member of Parliament

*"If I am not for myself,
who will be for me?*

*If I am only for myself,
what am I?*

If not now, when?"

Hillel

Preface

I have lived through wars and a revolution. One of the wars I volunteered for. I have had a gun held at my head, been kidnapped, been hit by a drunk driver and faced other life-threatening situations. All of this before I was 25 years old - but I am still here!

On the other hand, I also had many wonderful life-affirming experiences. I have been loved well and often. I have been spoiled, pampered and treated like a queen.

On the whole, I always felt that the glass was more often half-full than half-empty.

Having lived in Europe, the Middle-East and North America, my living accommodations ranged from six-to-a-room to a penthouse in New York overlooking Central Park.

I have been a daughter, sister, wife, mother - the whole catastrophe!

I have been rich and I have been poor - and rich *is* better!

This book is a combination of memories and advice. Like all advice books, this is highly idiosyncratic. Keep this in mind: what you are reading is one person's opinion. It is not the holy writ and none of it is written in stone. This is not the definitive tome on how to live your life. If something makes sense and applies to your life, well and good. If not, don't worry about it. My feelings won't be hurt. Bottom line: *take the best, leave the rest.*

After the holy books have been written and the great philosophers had their say, there isn't much that is new. I am reminded of a tag line on an old Hungarian comic magazine: "To a newborn babe, every joke is new." It is in this spirit that I offer you my thoughts. Some you have heard before, some might be new to you. My hope is that you will find something that will resonate within you and maybe something that you were not aware of or hadn't thought in quite the way it appears here.

I also hope to bring a smile to your face.

In closing let me say that I appreciate your picking up this book. It is my hope that you will find some of it useful. *Enjoy!*

Contents

Introduction

Let me tell you how and why this book came to be. Having lived on this planet for close to 60 years, I learned a few things in my time. I would like to share some of this with you. I don't have the corner on truth or a magic wand to make the problems of the world disappear. What I am offering is a smorgasbord of ideas based on my experiences.

Just so you know, I don't have academic qualifications on the subjects that I cover and I don't claim to have perfect or total information. I like to think that I am passing on common sense. I am presenting what I know up to this point in time and sharing this information in the hope that some of it might be useful to you. Look at it this way, if you pick up one useable idea, it's worth the price of the book. And if you find more good ideas, all the better. It's icing on the cake.

Let me start by saying that I am not going to tell you anything new. Everything I am going to tell you, you already know. It might not be all 'top of mind' awareness. You may not always be aware that you know it, but you really do. I see this book as a tool to help you access what you have stored away for future reference.

Compare reading this book to opening the files in your computer. Once you know the title, you'd be surprised at how much information there is, data you have entered and have since forgotten. This is an excuse for opening files and seeing what's in there. My role, basically, is to give you the name of the file and act as a guide in reminding you what's in the file. To help you retrieve and possibly look at the information with a new and different perspective.

At times there will be conflicting information in the different files. And at times you won't remember or will no longer agree with the content of some files. That's OK. You are at a different stage now than when you were keying in the information. Things change, people change.

Look at the data. What you agree with, keep. What no longer applies or doesn't make sense or you don't agree with, store on another disk, to be opened at another time. You would be surprised what comes up. Life is cyclical. Maybe next year it will make sense again, or the year after. I remember a wise friend telling me that you must not throw ideas away. Just store them for future recall.

If you find yourself coming up with what would appear to be mutually exclusive, opposing ideas, consider the Yin/Yang symbol. You will notice that inside the white part, there is a black centre and inside the black part, there is a white centre.

This is to remind us that out of darkness comes

light and out of light comes darkness. There can be no light without darkness and no darkness without light. No good without bad. In all bad things, there is a small piece of goodness. In all good things, there is a small part of bad.

Another way of looking at it might be that everything in life holds opposites within. A Mafia hit man might be a tender-hearted father and devoted husband. A saintly soul might have a dark side.

Consider the Zen view: they are two sides of the same coin. You cannot split the coin. It is what it is. This is the beginning of wisdom.

If something you read doesn't make sense or doesn't ring a bell, don't worry. Your intuition is the best radar. Maybe at some other point in your life it will make sense. Store it for future reference. Don't sweat it.

Look upon this book as a storehouse of ideas to consider. I am offering suggestions for a more balanced life. What works for one person might not work for someone else. It is up to you to decide what makes sense for you. You are the final judge. You know your own situation best. If it makes sense, use it with my blessing. If it doesn't, don't worry about it. My ego will not be shattered if some of my ideas don't find a home with you.

Mostly, I would like to spur you onto actions that will make your life more balanced, more enjoyable, more fun, more productive. Do only things that you want to do. To quote an old Hungarian saying: *"If you listen to me, you will do exactly as you wish."*

Consider this book a helpful guide. It is my belief that we are all on a journey of self-discovery. Some are ahead, some are behind. There are many ways to get to that mountain top. Your path might be different from mine or we might cross paths or travel in parallel paths.

Sometimes you have to make your own path. But, wherever you are in your journey, know this: there are people who have gone before you and people who will come after you.

With a bit of luck you might be able to find the markers left by those before you. And, if you are so inclined, maybe you can leave some markers for the people who follow you.

Most of all, it is my wish that you find some fellow travellers, soulmates, to share parts of the journey with you. People who are travelling with you for part of the journey, people who sometimes travel at your speed and who can help you. The longer you can make this stretch, the more fortunate you are.

Hopefully, when your travelling companion moves on, there will be other people who will share parts of the journey with you.

This book is dedicated to all my fellow travellers, past, present and future. May you have a pleasant journey and may you be blessed with wonderful travel companions.

I would like to thank all the people who attended my lectures and seminars over the years. Your ideas have been very helpful. It was a privilege to meet all of you. I learned a lot from you. I am reminded of the teacher who said:

"I learned a lot from my professors, more from my fellow students and the most from my pupils." So it has been with me. Thank you.

Alternative Medicine

a.k.a. Complementary
Holistic
Natural
Non-Invasive
Wholistic

*L*et me start by saying what this chapter is **NOT** - *it is NOT about bashing Western/conventional medicine.* It is about integrating the two systems. It is about getting the best of both worlds. It is giving you some options that you might not have been familiar with, options that will help put you in charge of your health.

Please remember that I am *not* against Western medicine. I am suggesting that we combine the two to our best advantage. For example, I am fortunate to have an excellent family doctor who has been my primary health-care giver for the past 25 years and will remain so. But, I also see holistic practitioners when it makes sense for me to do so. My family doctor is aware of this and has no problem with it.

(Not only is he not against them, he is knowledgeable about some of the complementary practices.

At times, he will share with me what some of his other patients have found useful and asks me what has worked for me. He is, in many ways, like an old-fashioned country doctor. He genuinely cares about his patients. He asks the questions that holistic practitioners ask; questions about emotional well-being, family and social issues, work-related problems. He returns phone calls promptly and follows up on test results as soon as he has them.)

At the time that this book is being written, about 50 percent of Canadians and Americans are using some form of alternative therapy. This is a staggering number of people in view of the fact that most of these therapies are not covered under most medical insurances and some of them are expensive.

What I would like to do in this chapter is to share with you some insights that I have gained by using many such practices over the past 15 years. Please keep in mind that you are getting a lay person's opinion - albeit, a reasonably well informed one. I have done extensive research as the writer and host of the television series: *"HEALTHY ALTERNATIVES - An Introduction to Complementary Practices & Lifestyle Choices."*

Conventional versus Alternative

Consider the merits of both conventional and complementary medicine. For example, if you have an accident, I would **not** suggest that you go to a chiropractor. Of course you should go to the nearest emergency room! *Then* follow it up with a visit to a chiropractor.

Western medicine is at its best in emergencies, accidents, blood tests, x-rays, complex testings, blood transfusion, organ transplants, surgeries, to name a few. On the other hand, alternative methods are effective in dealing with long-term, chronic conditions - conditions that have not responded to conventional treatments.

It has been suggested that, for some conditions, the body heals itself and the doctor gets paid. I rather like the ancient Chinese system - the doctor got paid if the patient got better. If the patient did not improve or died, the doctor did not get paid. Seems fair to me! (Somehow I don't think we can sell the idea to many medical associations, do you?)

It is up to each and every one of us to find the best medical help. Your health is the most important asset you have and yet it is not given the priority it deserves. People spend more time, energy and money on buying a car or a house than on their health. No car or house will be of much use to you if you are sick, or, God forbid, dead. *Just a bit of reality check, folks!* It is time to re-think our priorities.

Historical perspective

Most of us are familiar with the Western methods of dealing with our health. I would like to suggest some ideas why you might want to look at some of the other ways.

Some of the basic alternative philosophies are:
- First, do no harm
- Support the body's natural healing abilities
- Treat the patient, not the disease
- Treat the whole body
- Treat the cause, not the symptom
- Prevention

Most of the complementary ways have been around since mankind itself. Although I am not a betting woman, I would be willing to bet that there were no antibiotics in the Garden of Eden, but there were plants and flowers - and some with healing properties!

Traditional Chinese Medicine goes back thousands of years. Acupuncture, one of its branches, is currently used in some of the major hospitals in the U.S.A. and Canada. My personal acupuncturist works hand-in-hand with the western-trained specialist when her patients are undergoing surgery.

Native Indian and other folk healing systems have also been around for thousands of years. *Ayurvedic Medicine*, the traditional medicine of India, has seen a revival in North America in the last ten years or so, mostly because of the efforts of Deepak Chopra. When he was in my city recently, the tickets were snapped up within days and they were being scalped. There is obviously a great interest and need that he is responding to. (Somehow I don't think that a conventional doctor would fill too many 3000 seat auditoriums!)

Our ancestors knew the healing power of plants

and used them before antibiotics came on the scene. At the time that this books being written we have a serious problem with super germs - germs that don't respond to antibiotics. It might be interesting to contemplate the possibility of things coming full circle: going back to plants and flowers for their antibiotic properties. Food for thought, that!

It is up to each and every one of us to research both the conventional and alternative methods. It is your body, your responsibility, not your doctor's. Take control, take charge. Read up on your ailments. Nobody knows your body better than you and nobody has as much at stake as you in keeping it healthy. I am not suggesting that you do your own brain surgery or heart transplant. What I am suggesting is that you take responsibility and take care of yourself - body, mind and soul. It is your life.

Personal experiences

Let me share a few experiences I have had with alternative medicine. About 15 years ago I was in London, walking along Piccadilly and I had to stop to take a breath. I could not walk and breathe at the same time. I had a history of asthma, allergies and hayfever. I was a regular visitor to the emergency room at my local hospital. Somehow being on foreign soil really scared me. Even though the natives spoke English reasonably well(!), I was concerned about being in a strange hospital.

It was a sobering experience and when I returned to Canada, I decided to do something about my condition. I started on a journey of self-discovery and self-healing that has been on-going.

First I went to the specialist who was handling my case and asked what I could do about my condition. I was already on a number of steroid-based drugs and I was concerned about what the future held. The long and short of it was that he told me that I was progressing along a normal, expected course for someone with my history of allergies, hayfever and asthma. When I asked what would happen when the medications no longer worked, I was told that I could carry around a portable oxygen tank! This did not cheer me up one bit. I was not particularly overjoyed at the prospect of carrying an oxygen tank with me for the rest of my life.

I embarked on a six-month long research project. I set out to learn all I could about allergies, asthma and hayfever. Let me tell you, I was motivated and how! After all, this was *my* life we were talking about! First I researched the western views and then methodically checked out the alternative sources from A to Z. I looked at *Acupuncture, Aroma Therapy, Bach Flower Remedies, Bio-Feedback, Chiropractic, Energy Balancing, Herbal Remedies, Homeopathy, Naturopathy, Qi Kung, Tai Chi, Vegetarianism, Vitamins/ Supplements, Yoga and Zen Buddhism* - to name a few.

My research took many different forms. I read everything I could find. I attended lectures. I met with many alternative practitioners.

At the end of my research I came up with my own system for self-healing. I became vegetarian. I started taking Chinese herbs, practising yoga and meditation, exercising, getting plenty of rest, and drinking 6 - 8 glasses of water per day.

Within about 3 months I changed my lifestyle completely. Two weeks into my regime I was able to get off some of my medication and eventually ended up using minimal doses.

These changes affected other parts of my life. I used to go through bottles of aspirin for headaches. With the new regime, my headaches disappeared. I lost weight, had more energy and people told me I looked 10 years younger. My allergies seem to have disappeared, my asthma and hayfever are much less severe.

You might be interested to know that my late father referred to my hayfever as a rich person's sickness since I developed hayfever when I moved to Toronto (the hayfever capital of the world!) after my wedding. Marriage improved my financial status and my father said that when I lived in Montreal I was too poor to have hayfever. When I got married and got richer I could afford it!

One of the aspects of an asthma attack is that it can be brought on by emotional upsets. What was clear to me is this: *Emotional upset= asthma attack= shorter life.* Once I was aware of this, I was determined not to let things upset me. I worked out a system: whenever I felt that things were getting to me, I would stop and ask myself this question: *"Is it worth shortening my life over this issue?"* You'd be surprised how few issues are!

I had also suffered from yeast infections with alarming regularity prior to my lifestyle change. I went to see a nutritionist who told me that one cause might be a yeast imbalance in my system. This made sense to me. I cut out yeast from my diet, and presto! no more yeast infections - not one in the last 15 years.

Another one of my problems that has been solved by alternative methods was constipation. If this is an issue for you, you might consider adding 1 or 2 teaspoonfuls of flax seed (a.k.a. linseed) to your diet. Be sure you get the ground variety, or grind it yourself because if it is not ground, it will just go through your system and not aid the digestive process. This is a natural product that has additional benefits and it is cheaper than other laxatives. If you go to your local market, you can get enough for a dollar to last you 2 or 3 months. Now, that's what I call a bargain!

How alternative medicine works

Alternative practitioners look at the total body as an integrated system. When you go to a chiropractor with a headache, he will adjust your total spine, not just your neck. It stands to reason that when one vertebra is out of kilter, the whole spine needs adjusting.

When you have a cold, your whole system is down, not just your head, or chest or throat. And, by the way, when you have a cold, for heaven's sake, please stay home, don't give it to the rest of us. As hard as it is to accept, you are not irreplaceable. In case you are wondering where you fit into the larger picture, consider this: what would happen to the world at large if you stayed home for a week? Now, consider what would happen if a sanitation worker stayed home for a week! *(Just a little reality check!)*

When you have a cold, remember what your mother told you and follow her advice: stay in bed (alone!), drink plenty of liquid, eat chicken soup (Jewish penicillin) and other easy-to-digest foods. In case you are wondering, your mother is a very wise woman. The advice she gave you is solid and has been proven by research. This is a folk remedy and it works. If you went to an alternative practitioner, she might suggest adding garlic, onion, Vitamin C and B and Echinacea to your regime.

You are addressing your whole body and you are helping your body's natural healing ability by staying in bed, drinking and eating lightly. You are treating the cause, not the symptoms. Your body will repay you by getting well quickly.

Or you can try the ancient *Hungarian Hat Cure*. Put a hat at the foot of your bed. Go to bed, taking your favourite alcoholic beverage a with you and start drinking. When you see two hats, you are cured. Of course by then you don't really care, do you? Enjoy!

Alternative medicine is individualized. No one else has the same problems as you and you need individualized treatment. Of course there are some standard medications but the combination that an alternative practitioner will prescribe is tailored to your specific needs. Makes sense to me.

Holistic practitioners are user-friendly. They are committed to help you heal in the most effective way.

Your first visit may take about an hour to an hour and a half. You will be asked many questions about your mind, body and soul. The more they know about you, the more they are able to create a personal regime that will help.

They work with you in devising a health plan that you can live with. Not much use a doctor telling you to lose 20 pounds if they don't also tell you how to go about doing it in a way that you can live with and are willing to commit to.

In my experience, I have found the folks in the alternative health field to be open-minded, flexible, approachable and respectful of their patients' needs. Most of them specialize in more than one area, so they are able to use whichever methods would be the most useful for the patient. Also, if it is not their area of expertise, they will refer you to other health care professionals -alternative and traditional.

In Europe, alternative methods, especially Homeopathy, have been the medicine of choice for centuries. Most of the royal houses use homeopaths. The British Royal family has had homeopaths for generations. In America, for example, Henry Ford had a personal homeopath. It is interesting to consider that people who can afford any kind of medical attention chose alternative forms. Something to think about.

The issue of money

One of the biggest issues most of us face in wanting to consult with an alternative practitioner is money.

Most are not covered under most health plans or are only partially covered by some.

Here are some thoughts about the money issue. First, on a very basic level: if traditional medicine is not helping you, then I would suggest you don't have that many other options. This is your health we are talking about. As trite as it may be, if there is a will, there is a way.

Secondly, if you live in any fairly large urban centre, chances are there might be a training facility for the alternative therapist that you need. For example, I live in Toronto and I go to the Canadian College of Naturopathic Medicine where I see a student in her last year of training at a very reduced rate. I am getting excellent service, and at the same time, I am helping her in her practicum. Other friends of mine go to the Chiropractic College. Check out your area.

A third way of getting around the money issue is for you to be aware that alternative practitioners are very often open to creative financial solutions. Some may offer a "sliding" scale, some may be amenable for a "barter" arrangement. For example, I have marketing skills which I traded for getting acupuncture. At other times I was able to pay on an instalment plan. Tell your treatment giver that money is an issue and chances are you can work something out.

Finally, alternative medicine is also non-toxic, non-intrusive non-addictive and ecologically sound.

May you have a long & Healthy life!

Should you be so inclined, here are some suggestions you might consider:

★ Visit a health food store

★ Check out an alternative book store

★ Read up on your illnesses
   - both traditional and complementary

★ Attend a lecture on an alternative method that strikes your fancy

★ Ask your friends if they are seeing any natural healers

★ Consult a holistic practitioner

Goal Setting

Why Set Goals? Because if you don't know where you are going, how will you know when you get there? If you don't set goals for yourself, you can bet your life that someone else will. Would you rather make your own decisions or have someone else make them for you? I say it's your life and you're in control. You decide where you want to go and how to get there.

Know yourself / Be true to yourself

The first thing you might consider prior to setting goals is finding out who you are.

An un-examined life is not worth living. What an elegant and yet simple proposition. Simple, yes; easy, no. Find out who you are. You should be an expert on yourself. Who better? Take time to learn about fascinating YOU. There hasn't been and will never be anyone like you. (Unless, of course, you are a Trekkie, in which case *you know* there is alternate universe where your double exists! But I digress!)

Most people know more about their cars or their hobbies than they know about themselves. More's the pity. Take it on as a project. Pretend that you have to write a paper on yourself. Research it as if your life depended on it, as it might well. The more you know about yourself, the more you are able fulfill your dreams. Consider the importance of the assignment. When you don't know who you are, you spend a lot of energy trying to be somebody else. If, on the other hand, you know who you are, you are in the driver's seat. And, of course, once you know who you are, it is much easier to be true to yourself.

How do you find out who you are? Here is an exercise you might try.

> *You have six months to live.* You are healthy and you have sufficient money. What would you do if you knew with certainty that you only have six months? What would you do differently? What would you keep on doing as you always have?

Look at your answers very carefully. Does anything surprise you? Anything you want to change? Now is the time!

Mission statement

Before you decide on your goals, you might also want to look at the *big picture* of your life. This your 'raison d'être' for being on this planet, your mission, if you will.

How do you arrive at a personal mission statement? If you have participated in writing one at your place of work, then use that process. If you haven't done it before, don't worry, it's not rocket science. Do some soul searching and ask yourself some probing questions as to who you are, where you are and where you want to be.

There are no hard and fast rules. Just close your eyes and imagine being all that you can and want to be and write it down. Think about it for a couple of weeks and if you still like what you wrote, then make it official.

This is not a task that you want to rush. After all, this is *your life* we are talking about! So take your time and do as good a job of it as you can.

To start you on your way, let me share my personal mission statement.

> *My mission in life is to make a difference, to leave the world a better place than the one I was born into. I use humour and a pragmatic, down-to-earth approach in my writings and public speaking to teach people living skills that will help them lead less stressful, happier, more productive and balanced lives.*

I wrote this about five years ago and it still works for me. You can change yours whenever you have reached your goals and are ready to write a new mission statement and new goals. Good luck.

SETTING GOALS

When you are setting goals it might be helpful *to plan as if you were to live forever and act as if today was your last day on earth.* This is not as contradictory as it may sound. In your planning, reach for the moon. In your every day actions, do all you can to achieve your long-term goals.

It would be beneficial to start with the desired end result and work backwards. One way to set goals for yourself is to consider: what would you like to see carved on your tombstone? Start working towards that goal today.

There is a Chinese saying: "The longest journey begins with one step." So, if you would like to be a concert pianist, you might start by practising and listening to all the great concert pianists. (There is a story of someone in New York asking how to get to Carnegie Hall. The response: *"Practice! Practice! Practice!"*)

If you would like to be the President of the United States, you might start by majoring in Political Science or working for your local candidate in the next election.

If you want to be a millionaire, look at how other people made big money and see if you can emulate them.

You get the general idea. You have to have a goal and then make a plan to reach it. Keep in mind: if you can *conceive* it and *believe* it, you can *achieve* it.

Identify personal and career goals

One of the biggest problems with goal setting, in my experience, is that people choose career goals that are contrary to their personal goals.

For example, let's say, you want to be a top salesman for an international company, a job that involves extensive travel. It would be very difficult, at the same time, to be a model husband and father. You might not be able to go to the Little League games or piano recitals or be home for your anniversary or your wife's birthday.

I am not suggesting that top international salesmen don't make good parents or spouses. All I am voicing here is an opinion that if your number one priority is to be the top salesman, then something else will have to suffer. As the old saying goes: *"You cannot dance at two weddings at the same time."*

Personality traits and family history

Another consideration might be where your natural talents lay. If you are a shy, introverted loner, then being a social director might not be the ideal position for you.

Now, of course, people can and do change. But if you are going against your natural bent, you are wasting a lot of energy. You might consider doing something that is more in line with your natural talents.

Another issue you might look at: *why* have you chosen the goal that you chose? For example, have the people in your family always been doctors? lawyers? politicians? rum-runners?

Family tradition is not necessarily the best way to pick your goals. If you have the talent and the desire for it, by all means, go for it. But *do not,* I repeat, *do not* base your life on becoming a doctor *only* because that is what your family expects you to do.

You are unique, your talents are unique and your

needs are unique. You are *not* your parents or your grandparents. Whatever goal you set for yourself, make sure it is *your* goal. Something that you are passionate about. Not something that is expected of you. This is the 21st Century, not the Middle Ages. You owe it to yourself to be true to yourself. Otherwise, as Humphrey Bogart said in *Casablanca*: "You will regret it. Maybe not today, maybe not tomorrow, but soon and for the rest of your life."

After you have identified your business and personal goals, look at the final outcome that you want. What you want to be remembered for. Everyone has some special talents that they bring to the world. Some people have more than one. There is a Buddhist saying: *"If you have the ability, you have the responsibility."*

As you think of your goals, remind yourself that it is your life. You will have to live with the consequences of your decision - for better or for worse. Choose carefully.

The past

When setting goals, it might be wise to look at the past. You may want to look at your past achievements. List the things that you are particularly pleased with. Chances are that what pleased you in the past will also please you in the future.

For example, I have always enjoyed being in the limelight. My earliest, most vivid and joyful memory is being a princess in a kindergarten play when I was 3 or 4 years old. After more than 50 years, I can still tell you the colour of my outfit, my tiara and my magic wand.

Most of my subsequent achievements had an element of being in the public eye. My natural talents and desires have been to try to make people laugh, think or help them improve their lives. I now do this by having a television series, writing this book, doing seminars and delivering keynote speeches.

Look at your past before you decide on your future course. If you have the time and the inclination, you might want to write a detailed list of your accomplishments. But remember, list only accomplishments that you are proud of, those that brought you personal satisfaction and joy.

For example, I am proud of getting my B.A. as a mature student. Proud because I earned my degree after being away from school for more than twenty years, without having gone to high school and doing it while travelling across Canada with my husband and small daughter.

I followed my husband to different cities and took courses that would fit in with his assignments in each city: Ottawa, Toronto, Calgary, Vancouver and Victoria. I went to school while I travelled, played hostess, was a mother and wife. So, for me, my B.A. is a badge of honour. I worked hard for it and I am proud of it. (Almost as proud as of my tiara and magic wand!)

The present

Now that you have looked at your past, look at your present. Where are you in the scheme of things? Your personal life? Your business life? What changes do you have to make to achieve your goals? Are you able to make those changes? Are they worth the sacrifices you would have to make? Take a long, hard look at your answers.

I remember when I went back to school. I was considering going to law school. Since I think I am articulate and, at times, persuasive, I thought, "Aha, I'll become a lawyer." And, let me tell you, the idea really appealed to me.

I also had a lot of support from family and friends. Everyone thought I'd make a great lawyer, except for my daughter, who was two or three at the time. When I told her that I was going to be a lawyer, she looked at me and said: "Don't be silly, only men can be lawyers!" And from her perspective, that made sense. The only lawyers she knew were men! My then-husband talked about being married to the first woman supreme court judge!

Just as I started the process, my husband (a wise man) said: "Have you considered how difficult this will be? The hours that you will have to spend studying? The time that you will have to take away from family?" His questions gave me pause. In truth, I had not considered the trade offs that I would have to make. On giving it more serious consideration, I decided against law school.

In retrospect, it was the right decision. As I look at the lawyers that I know, there is no doubt in my mind that I would not have been willing to work as hard as they did, either in law school or afterwards. By nature I am not a workaholic nor am I a type "A" personality. These seem to be important attributes for successful lawyers.

The future

Now that you have considered the past and the present, look to the future. The goal that you have picked for yourself, is it truly what you want? Would it make you happy? Something that you are passionate about? Be careful what you wish for, you might get it.

Think carefully. It would be a shame to get to the end of the line only to find out that this was not what you *really* wanted. Take your time. Consider this a research project. Give it the time and energy it needs.

If you are not sure, ask yourself: what would it be if I was sure? You'd be surprised what you might find if you dig deep enough.

As I mentioned earlier, the idea of being a lawyer really appealed to me. I felt that I had the talents and abilities to be a good one. But in reality, I was not interested in working that hard either in school or at work. I loved being a mother and wife and I was not willing to give that up.

So look at what you want. Look at what you have to give up to get it. Be very sure. It's like leaning a ladder against a building and finding out when you get to the top you are at the wrong window! Take your time. You are worth it. And do it now. As Hillel said: *"If not now, when?"*

Good luck!
May you reach your goals!

Suggested next steps:

★ Write your mission statement.

★ Do a goal setting exercise. You can find many excellent reference books in your local library or book store. Here is a simplified version for your consideration.

a. set your goals

b. set up timetables, working backwards: things I want to achieve...
   - before I die
   - within 20 years
   - within 15 years
   - within 10 years... etc, etc.

c. break it down to manageable tasks. For example, in writing this book, my end goal was to write a book. I broke this down to so many chapters per week, so many pages per day.

d. put it in writing. There is something about putting things down on paper that will act as a motivater for most people. Having said that, if you find that you work best by *not* having a detailed blueprint and that you do your best work by flying by the seat-of-your-pants, then by all means, do what works for you.

★ If you are a visual person, and you are so inclined, there is a fun project to help you in goal setting. It is called the TREASURE MAP. Here is what you do: collect a number of magazines. Look through them and cut out pictures of things that you would like to have in your life. If you cannot find what you want, draw or write it out. There are no hard and fast rules. We are doing this for fun. Don't worry about money. Whatever appeals to you, cut it out. Paste it on a large cardboard or on several smaller sheets.

Some people take pictures and put them on their fridge. Others carry them around with them. It doesn't matter. Whatever you are comfortable with. I keep mine in a scrapbook and look at it occasionally and I am always pleasantly surprised at the goals that I have achieved. Do whatever makes sense for you, whatever pleases you. *Enjoy!*

Happiness Is...

*P*eople are as happy as they allow themselves to be. Strange but true. I'm not suggesting that you wake up in the morning and say: "today I will be happy" - although I can't think of a better way to start your day! It is much more subtle than that.

First, you have to *know* what makes you happy. Then you have to *give yourself permission* to be happy. And, finally, you actually have to *do* what makes you happy. A three-step process, with each step being important.

There is a wonderful Yiddish saying: *"Happiness is found not in getting what you want but wanting what you have."* I always found this to be a particularly comforting thought. Another idea to consider: if your needs are not met, drop your needs!

Genes

Yes, you do have "happy" genes. Some of us have more, some of us have fewer. It's the luck of the draw of what you get from the genetic lottery. You can thank your lucky stars or curse your misfortune, but it is a given, like being tall or short, fat or skinny.

There have been many experiments done with twins who were separated at birth and were brought up with very different sets of parents. What the studies indicate is that as adults, their levels of happiness/unhappiness were the same regardless of the differences in parenting.

The good news is that it is only *one* of the many deciding factors. If you were born with less than your fair share, you have to work a bit harder, but it is not an insurmountable obstacle in your quest for a happier life.

Your Choice

Yes, it is your choice. It is your decision to be happy. It is indeed your duty. It is enshrined in the American Constitution. So what if you're not an American? Elect yourself an honourary citizen and abide by the Constitution. Easy as (American Apple) pie!

Journey, not a destination

Happiness is not some hotel you can check into. It is not some place you arrive at the end of some journey. It is a mode of travelling. You know, getting there being half the fun.

It could be a solitary journey or you can have travelling companions. I have always envisioned it as people travelling on different roads in the same general direction. In my imagination there are people ahead of you. People who are a sort of role models and guides, telling you what to watch out for, warning you of dangers ahead. And there are people behind you for whom you are the role model and guide.

If you are lucky, you will find soul mates along the way. People who will share parts of the journey with you. If you are very lucky, they may stay with you for most or all of the journey.

A Purposeful Life

One of the ways to achieve happiness is to live a purposeful life. A life that has meaning beyond your own needs. You are here for a purpose. Your assignment, should you chose to accept it - is to find your purpose. In searching and fulfilling that purpose you are making your contribution to the common good.

It has always been my hope that at the end of my life I could look back on my achievements and be able to say that my being on this planet has made a difference, and that I am leaving it a better place than I found it.

Balanced Lifestyle

A balanced lifestyle will go a long way towards a happier you. Balance between the different spheres of your life: physical, mental, emotional, spiritual. As well as balance within each area.

Imagine your life as a wheel. Think of the different aspects: physical, mental, emotional, spiritual as spokes of the wheel. Now imagine that the spokes are of different lengths - you get a wobbly wheel. Difficult to make it roll smoothly. On the other hand, if all the spokes are the same length you get a perfectly balanced wheel that rolls easily and effortlessly.

Meaningful Relationships

Meaningful relationships are to be treasured. To have people in your life with whom you can be yourself is a blessing. I always thought that the most important things in life are relationships. When you connect with someone on a heart-to-heart level, that's my idea of bliss. The more of these relationships that you have in your life, the more fulfilled and happy you will be.

Attitude of Gratitude

An attitude of gratitude goes a long way towards achieving happiness. A grateful heart makes you a happier person. You have so much to be grateful for. Make a list of the things that you are blessed with. You can start at either end of the spectrum, go from the highly personal to the more global, or work it the other way. For example, my list might look like this:

I am grateful for living:
- this time of history rather than the Middle Ages
- in a democratic country with many freedoms
- in a country with medicare and four seasons
- in Toronto, a city that is safe and clean

I am grateful for:
- being healthy
- having a roof over my head
- being vegetarian
- being able to exercise
- being able to write this book

...you get the idea! You have a lot to be thankful for.

A grateful heart makes it easier to deal with life's problems. And, you know we all have problems. The trick is to be glad for what you have and be grateful for it. Now, I am not suggesting for a moment that you should not aim for better and higher. Your aim should exceed your reach. I am only suggesting that you already have so many things in your life to be grateful for and it might be a good idea to acknowledge it. You'll be a happier person for it.

Positive and Negative People

As the song says: *"You've gotta accentuate the positive, eliminate the negative"*. Not a bad summing up of the kind of people you want in your life. Hanging out with positive folks will lift your spirits. Do your best to get rid of toxic people in your life. They will bring you down, contaminate you, make you unhappy. You deserve to be around up-beat, happy people. People who light up the room when they enter. People who are like rays of sunshine. Flowers and plants all turn towards the sun. Surely, human beings ought to do the same!

Pampering yourself

Now that you have balance in your life, you are practising an attitude of gratitude, you have gotten rid of all the toxic people in your life, it is time to be *really* good to yourself. Pamper yourself. That's right. It is your right, *indeed your duty* to be good to yourself. Not only is this not selfish, it is downright altruistic! That's right, altruistic.

When you are happy, you can share your happiness with others. Think of yourself as a vessel filled with a wonderful substance. If you pour all this wonderful substance out and don't refill it, you will be left with an empty vessel. If, on the other hand, you keep on replenishing it, you will always be able to share with others.

If your vessel is empty, you are not able to give to others. What you don't have, you cannot give. Therefore, it is your duty to look after yourself, to keep yourself filled with all the things that keep you going, physically, mentally, emotionally and spiritually so that you *can* help others.

Of course, I am not advocating unreasonable selfishness and self-centredness. I am talking about balance. If you work around the clock seven days a week you won't have time for replenishment of any kind. If you volunteer every night of the week, you won't have time for your family. If you exercise around the clock... well, you get the idea. Everything in moderation.

In our society one of the biggest problems for many of us is to give ourselves permission to replenish ourselves. And, not only the permission, but to find the time to do it.

Here are some of ideas for you to consider. On the issue of time: Whenever someone tells me that they haven't got time for themselves, I always point out (not too unkindly, I hope) that they have the same amount of time as Mother Teresa or Einstein or the President of the United States: 24 hours a day, seven days a week. We are all allotted the same amount of time, it's what we do with it that counts.

Secondly, if you are not taking time for yourself whether it is to exercise, have a proper diet, get enough sleep or time to meditate - it's like driving a car and not stopping for gas. Eventually both you and the car will run out of gas.

The "Not So" Stern Rule

If you resolved the time issue (Congratulations!) but are still struggling with the permission thing, have no fear, help is on the way! Following is *The "Not So" Stern Rule* to consult when you want to do something and you are not sure if you should, especially if you feel that it is self-indulgent. (And, by the way, there is nothing wrong with a little self-indulgence every now and then!)

Ask yourself the following three questions:
1. Is it against the law?
2. Will anyone, including myself, get hurt?
3. Am I able and willing to deal with the consequences?

If you can honestly answer *NO* to questions one and two and *YES* to number three, then you are free to follow your heart's desire. And that's *The "Not So" Stern Rule*. If anyone objects, just say: "Susan said I could!" And, indeed, *YOU CAN!*

Don't worry! Be happy!

*Suggestions for your quest for
happiness journey:*

★ Make a list of at least 25 things that make
  you happy and ask yourself the following
  questions:
  - When was the last time I did them?
    Today, last week, last month, last year?
    How often?
    If you don't like your answers,
    do something about it!

★ Make a personal "*Happy Tape*"
  - tape songs, poems, sayings that make you
  happy and listen to it whenever your spirit
  needs lifting

★ Hang out with positive people, people
  who make you feel glad to be alive

★ Think of the glass as half full rather than
  half empty

Humour & Laughter

"Laughter is the best medicine" - truer words were never spoken! As long as you can laugh, things are looking up. As far as it being a medicine, in fact it is. When you laugh, your body produces endorphin, the "feel good" chemical that has many clinically-proven positive effects.

You might be interested to know that research indicates that optimists live longer and have a better time of it. I am more than happy to buy into this theory. It makes sense to me at a gut level and if there are studies to support it - that's good enough for me!

One of the strongest advocates of laughter and humour as a healing method is Norman Cousins. In his book, *"Anatomy of an Illness"* (a book highly recommended!) he recounts his experiences in dealing with a serious illness by introducing a lot of levity as part of his healing regime. He found that by watching Marx Brothers movies (highly recommended), he was getting better quicker.

And while there was no scientific double-blind study at the time, (after all there was only one

Norman Cousins), for my money, it is good enough that he said it worked for him.

There have been many studies that support the idea that laughter is good for us whether we are well or ill. (Speaking of "well", there is an old vaudeville routine about a doctor who falls into a well and hurts himself. Punch line: "He should have attended to the sick and left the well alone!")

Some enlightened corporations provide "laugh breaks" for their employees. There are also courses given on the importance of humour and laughter. You know that when corporations pay good money it is because it improves the bottom line. So, if your employer is not providing you with such opportunities, make your own opportunity and laugh without the benefit of formal training.

Have a belly laugh every day for 30 seconds. I mean a roaring, shake your booties, let it all hang out kind of belly laugh. Do it right now. I'll wait. Don't you feel better now? Of course you do.

It takes fewer muscles to smile than to frown and we all look better when we smile. Just look at yourself in the mirror. Try frowning and then try smiling. Which do you like better? No wonder the photographers always tell us to smile when they are taking our pictures. After all, they want us to like their masterpieces of us, and if we are smiling, chances are we will!

I remember working for a man with a granite face and a personality to go with it. He was a difficult person and most of the staff were afraid of him.

When I first started working for him, I made him laugh and I was amazed at the transformation. He looked like a different person. When he smiled his whole face lit up. And unlike most people, he also smiled with his eyes. You know how most people smile only with their mouth and the rest of their face doesn't move! Not Old Granite Face. He smiled with his whole face, and it was a joy to behold. From then on, I tried very hard to make him smile and occasionally I even succeeded. Wherever he is, I hope he is smiling.

Smiling re-enforces the positive side of yourself. The side that you want to nourish. The side you want the world to see more of. And, smiling doesn't cost any money. As a matter of fact, a lot of people earn lots of money by smiling. Think of all the commercials with those toothy, smiling models! And good money is being made by those who make us smile. Think of the TV series: *TV Bloopers, Funniest Videos, Candid Camera, Kids Say The Darndest Things...* etc, etc. And all those comic strips - the first thing I turn to in my daily newspaper! Think of clowns and comedians - making a good living by making us laugh. There's gold in them thar laughs!

If you don't smile that often, consider smiling more. If things are too grim, force yourself, *"fake it till you make it!"* And if you are feeling good, for goodness sake, notify your face and smile.

I am not suggesting that you go around grinning all the time like the village idiot! Of course not. They would lock you up and throw away the key. There are times when smiling is inappropriate. But more often than not, it's OK to smile.

One of my most embarrassing moments involved inappropriate laughter. In the 1960's I worked for an oil distributor in Montreal. My supervisor was the boss' niece, Miss Cohen. She was an elderly spinster lady. Among other things, she used to talk to herself - out loud. I remember once asking her why she talked to herself and she replied, without any irony and with the utmost sincerity and honesty, that if she wanted intelligent conversation she had to talk to herself. But I digress.

We worked on the second floor of a building with rickety wooden stairs. One fine day, as she was going down, she slipped and rolled down the stairs. As luck would have it, she was not badly hurt, although I suspect her ego might have taken a beating. As I stood at the top of the stairs looking down, hard as I tried, I could not stop laughing. There was something highly amusing about watching a human body roll down like a rag doll. But it was not a good time to laugh!

One of the things that I do to ensure that I have lots of humour and laughter in my life is to collect amusing sayings. Following are some of my favourites:

"She who laughs LASTS" Hungarian saying

"Laughter is time spent with the gods" Japanese proverb

"Laughter is the shortest distance between two people"

I also have a large collection of comic strips and several personal comic audio cassettes. I record my favourite comic songs and verses and listen to them whenever my spirits need lifting. Try it, you'll like it!

My library also contains a large section of books and magazines that I find amusing. These include books of comedies, comic verse, humorous anecdotes and satirical drawings.

Check out your local library for books, tapes, videos and magazines that tickle your funny bones. Used book stores, garage sales and flea markets are also a treasure trove.

A couple of my favourites: (no, I don't have any financial interest in either of them, I just like them)

Ashleigh Brilliant - all of his books are wonderful.
   If you can't find it in your book store or
   library, you can write to him:
Ashleigh Brilliant
117 West Valerio Santa Barbara CA 93101

Going Bonkers? - a gem of a magazine
   Going Bonkers?
   P.O. Box 189, Palm Beach FL 33480

Smile and the world smiles with you!

*Suggestions for getting more levity
into your life:*

★ Make your own "Gallery of Gaiety"
  of comic strips

★ Have a belly laugh every day

★ Make your own "Laugh Tape"

★ Start or enlarge the "Comic" section of
  your library

Lifestyle Choices

As you go through life you will find that some things are within your power and some things are not. Fortunate is the person who is able to make this distinction quickly and easily and then make decisions based on this knowledge.

If you need a reminder, let me quote the Serenity Prayer:

> **God grant me the SERENITY to accept the things I cannot change, COURAGE to change the things that I can and the WISDOM to know the difference.**

Of all the things that are within your power, there is nothing else as decisive, and with such far-reaching effects, as the lifestyle choices that you make on a daily basis. By lifestyle choices I mean the everyday big and small decisions that you make.

Lifestyle choices fall into the following categories: physical, mental, emotional and spiritual. There are some overlaps, so let's not be too hidebound by categories.

Physical: how you look after your body. This could range from your commitment to environmental issues to your diet, sleeping and exercise regime

Mental: how you keep your grey cells functioning

Soulwork: how you nourish your soul

PHYSICAL

The environment

Let's start with the big picture. Are you aware of the ecological consequences of your actions? Do you live in harmony with Mother Nature? Are you working towards saving our environment? Just some questions you might ask yourself. You *know* what you are supposed to be doing; are you doing it? Yes, you are responsible, and yes there is a lot that one person *can* do.

If you are looking for guidance on how to be environmentally responsible, check with any local environmental group or your public library. You might keep in mind the three R's: REDUCE, RE-USE, RECYCLE.

Diet/Nutrition

I am not going to tell you anything you don't already know. Your mother and grandmother are/were right! Eat your greens. Eat a varied diet. Eat lots of fruit and vegetables. Drink lots of water. Go easy on sweets and animal fats. Increase whole grains. These are some of the basics of a good diet.

You can get some excellent advice from dieticians, nutritionists and alternative health care professionals. There are also courses being offered at community colleges.

In addition to your mother's good advice and what common sense tells you about diet, I would add one more suggestion: if your budget allows, buy organic fruits and vegetables. I know that organic is expensive, but remember, your body is a temple; you might want to watch what goes in there. And, of course, there is the *"you are what you eat"* school of thought. Organic food is healthier because there are no pesticides used and you are getting more of the essential minerals.

If organic is not within your budget, buy fresh, local produce. Next: buy frozen; and lastly: canned. This is the scale you might keep in mind as far as nutritional value is concerned. The most nutritious would be local organic produce and at the bottom are the canned varieties.

If you are able to, buy locally grown produce. These fruits and vegetables have shorter distances to get to you, therefore more of the nutrients remain. It might also be cheaper since the transportation costs should be lower.

Some schools of thought believe that by eating locally grown fruits and vegetables you are in harmony with nature around you. The same goes for seasonal fruits and vegetables. Also, you are supporting local farmers.

In addition to following a balanced diet, you might consider vitamins and supplements, even if your doctor tells you that if you have a balanced diet you don't need them. Consider this: unless your doctor is a recent graduate, she had no nutritional training in medical school. Unless she has studied nutrition after leaving medical school, she knows as much about nutrition as a well-informed lay person. Her advice is probably as good as anything you can find out for yourself in the current literature.

Having a balanced diet might have been the answer in the past, it is not true today. If you eat organic, you are improving your odds. But unless everything you eat is organic, you only drink purified water, you breathe purified air, and have no stress in your life - you need additional support.

One idea you might consider: becoming a vegetarian both for your own sake and for the sake of the planet. If not, how about cutting back on animal products. You will feel better, I guarantee. You will have fewer diseases and live longer. Listen to Oprah!

One more word about diet: drink lots of liquid. Preferably purified spring water. Coffee and soft drinks don't count! As a matter of fact, if you drink them, increase your water intake. The suggested water consumption is 1 litre for every 100 lbs. And before we leave the area of what we put into our bodies: consider cutting back on smoking and drinking.

Exercise and rest

Yes, you must exercise, there are no two ways about it.

Yes, I know there are people who don't and they are doing fine. Apparently, (if you can believe *People Magazine*) Paul Newman is one of these people. To add insult to injury, he supposedly drinks beer and is still in terrific shape. Mr. Newman, and the other lucky folks like him, can thank their lucky stars for their genetic heritage. For the rest of us, the bottom line is: *you must exercise!*

There are countless research projects that prove the efficacy of exercise in preventing many major diseases and helping us live longer and happier lives.

Exercise covers the gamut from aerobics to yoga. You don't have to join an expensive club or buy top-of-the line exercises machines - although, if you have the bucks, go for it!

The important thing is to find something that you *like* to do and that you stay with it! Set up a schedule, and keep to it. If you can, find someone to do it with you. If possible, do something outdoors. The stairmaster, stationary bike or indoor track are fine, but being outside sure beats being inside. You can appreciate nature and breathe fresh air.

When you are trying to decide what exercise to choose, remember that your choices are unlimited. My personal favourite is walking. Doesn't cost anything. Anyone can do it at any age, anywhere, anytime. And it's fun. Some others: bicycling, swimming, gardening, dancing, making love, doing house work, yoga, tai chi, hiking...the list goes on and on. As the ad says: JUST DO IT!

Before we leave the physical side of things, don't forget the importance of getting sufficient rest. You need rest to give your body a chance to recuperate physically, mentally and emotionally. This is the time your cells get replenished. This is the time to let go and let your body do its work.

Unfortunately in today's society, with our busy schedules, the first casualty seem to be sleep. It is a great misfortune. Your body needs to be recharged, and the best and most efficient way is sleep. When people tell me that they don't have time for sleep, I always remind them of the car and fuel analogy - if you don't put fuel in, it will stop running. Like exercise and food, sleep is one of the body's fuels. It is not a luxury, it is a necessity. *Watching television is optional, sleeping is essential!*

Just like any well-functioning machine, our body likes order. If you are able to, go to bed at the same time and get up at the same time. And if your schedule allows, take cat naps. If you have travelled to some countries where siesta is part of the routine, then you know how refreshing it can be.

MENTAL

How do you stay mentally alert? Like exercise, this is a major part of being healthy and living to a ripe old age and enjoying the journey. And there are tons of research results to indicate the importance of keeping your grey cells working. The secret of keeping your mental agility: *use it or lose it!* That's it, folks! Find out what gives you the most pleasure and do it.

Some possibilities:
- read
- write
- take a course
- give a course
- play chess
- do crossword puzzles - my personal favourite!
- learn new skills
- learn a new language
- travel
- play cards
- keep a journal

This is just to get you started! Make up your own list.

SOULWORK

So far so good. You are environmentally responsible, have an excellent diet, you exercise regularly, get plenty of rest and keep your grey cells working. Now let's get to the heart of the matter: your emotional and spiritual well-being.

Sadly, this is one of the most neglected areas, but there are signs that this is changing. According to recent research, people are returning to their religious roots and/or are searching for spiritual guidance.

I am not here to advocate any particular religion. This is a very personal choice and it is for you to make. However, I would suggest that, in addition to the religion that you were born and brought up in, you might consider reading up on some other religions, purely as a research project. You would be surprised at the similarities. For example, all of the major religions have their own version of the GOLDEN RULE. (There is also a *Platinum Rule*: Do unto others as *they* would wish to be done to.) Most of them also subscribe to some variation on THE TEN COMMANDMENTS.

However you replenish your emotional/ spiritual/ religious being, keep on doing it.

If you are not practising anything in this realm, consider doing something, anything, that you are comfortable with. It has now been scientifically proven that praying is good for you. Many studies indicate that people who pray, and are prayed for during illness, have fewer post-surgery complications and heal more quickly. People who pray also live longer and happier lives.

In addition to praying, let me share a personal practice I find soul-nourishing. On my birthday I send out letters of appreciation to people who have been special, people who have made a difference during the previous year. I thank them for being in my life and describe how they enriched my life. Wouldn't it be wonderful to receive such a letter? Maybe we can make it a global ritual. How about it?

Follow your bliss!

Some ideas you might consider:

★ Reduce, re-use, recycle

★ Visit a nutritionist

★ Do *one* thing to improve your diet

★ Start an exercise program

★ Make sure you get enough rest

★ Get a hobby that keeps your mind alert

★ Give some thought to your emotional/ spiritual life

Looking for Love in all the Right Places

*I*f you are currently in a committed, satisfactory relationship, skip this chapter. It is for folks who are between relationships and are looking for that special someone.

This is a three-parter:

Part One: Relationships
Part Two: Where to meet that special someone
Part Three: My adventures in the "Personals"

PART ONE: Relationships

I have some good news and some bad news. The good news is that if you had good relationships in the past, there's no reason why you can't have them again. And if you've had some not so good relationships, presumably you learned lessons from them. All for the good.

And now, some not so good news - at least for some of us more mature women. The numbers are against us. First, women live longer. There are more of us and fewer of them. Second, older men have the whole spectrum of women to choose from: from nubile young things to us wiser, more seasoned women.

While society accepts "trophy" wives as a fact of life, I've yet to hear much talk about "trophy" husbands. An older man who has a wife who is young enough to be his daughter doesn't even merit a second glance. But just imagine the reverse, an older woman with a much younger man and boy, oh boy, you set the tongues a-wagging.

But enough of that. My message to ladies of more mature persuasion: we are *"saging"* not aging. We are not getting older, we are getting better, like expensive vintage wine.

And now back to the matter at hand for all of us: *the why's and wherefore's of relationships.*

Your most important relationship

This is, of course, your relationship with yourself. You are the one person who is a constant. You are always there. You can travel the globe and wherever you go, there you are. You can never ever get away from yourself.

You must first learn to love yourself before you are ready for anyone else to love you. If you don't love yourself, how do you expect other people to love you? Would you love someone who did not love him- or herself?

If you don't know how to love yourself, how would you know how to love someone else? You cannot give what you haven't got.

If this is an issue for you, work on it. There isn't much chance of your making a go of any relationship until you have sorted this out. Remember, you are worth it. This is your life. Make the most of it.

Who are you?

If you don't know who you are, then how can you possibly know what kind of person you would like in your life? If you don't know what your needs are in a relationship, then anyone will do. Other people will make up your mind for you and that would be a shame.

You might start by looking back on your past relationships and examine what worked and what did not. Be brutally honest with yourself. No one else will see this, so there's no need for gilding the lily. And, if you are not completely honest, it's a waste of time.

List your past relationships and analyze them. Look at the strengths and weaknesses. Based on your past experience, decide what is important for you in a relationship. You might want to make two columns: what is important and what is not.

For example, my list would look like this:

Not important: age, looks, money/lack of, nationality

Important:
non-smoker, bright, sense of humour, romantic, emotionally mature, no small children, generousity of spirit, open mind, active, articulate, likes himself, urban/e

So, if you know someone like that, *please drop me a note!*

Do opposites attract?

Conventional wisdom has it that opposites attract. That might well be true, but do they live happily ever after? That, to me, would be the more compelling question. I have no statistics to back me up on this, but my common sense tells me that opposites may attract but I would doubt the staying power of the attraction.

The more you have in common, the better your chances of building a strong, long-term, positive relationship.

On a recent Barbara Walters show, Sophia Loren was asked why she married Carlo Ponti instead of Cary Grant. Her reply was: "I married Carlo because *he is of my world.*" [Italics are mine.] I have been a fan of Sophia Loren as an actress for a long time and this remark made me respect her as a person. She was right, of course. Cary Grant may have been one of the sexiest men in the world, but Carlo Ponti was of *her* world. And by all accounts, theirs is a happy and enduring marriage.

I was in a relationship with someone who was different from me. He had a theory that we should get to know each other's likes. One of our areas of differences was our taste in entertainment. He proposed that I come to one of his favourites and he, in turn, would come to one of mine. It was agreed.

His choice was a rock concert. I am more of a Noel Coward/Cole Porter/Broadway kind of person. However a deal is a deal and off we went to Maple

Leaf Gardens. Not one of my usual haunts. When we got there the air was thick and blue and fragrant. You did not have to bring your own stuff - just one deep breath and you were feeling no pain.

The show started. My ear drums were pierced by a woman on stage screeching at the top of her lungs. She was clad in a black leather outfit that she was poured into. The show consisted of her prancing around, making rude gestures and screeching some more. Needless to say it was my first and last rock concert!

But my friend was persistent and he wanted to accompany me to something that I enjoyed. I suggested Vera Lynn. He said, and I quote: "What's a veralin?" To his credit, he did come to hear Vera Lynn and was much more gracious about it than I was about the rock concert. Obviously not a match made in heaven.

Sex

When should sex enter a relationship? Later rather than sooner. Sex tends to cloud things. Give the relationship a chance. Falling in love should be like partaking of a superbly aged wine in an exquisite crystal glass. Take time to admire the glass. See how the light plays on the crystal. Drink in the aroma before you finally take a sip. Sip slowly and savour every minute. There is no hurry. The sweet anticipation will make it all the more pleasurable when your lips taste the wine and each other.

Office romance

Not a great idea. It is disruptive. It lowers morale. No matter how careful you think you are, people will find out. When it's over, one of you will want to leave. It's a losing proposition all around.

I worked for a large multi-national company where the vice-president was in a relationship with one of the managers. They were both single and it was certainly their right to enjoy each other's company. However, it played havoc on many levels. Productivity suffered because the other managers were afraid to say anything to her for fear that it would get back to the vice-president. She was ostracized and was not able to work effectively. Eventually they got married and she quit working.

Adultery

Don't go there. It's not good for you. When Cecil B. deMille was making the film *The Ten Commandments*, he said: *"You cannot break a commandment. You can only break yourself against it."* Something to think about.

You get hurt. You hurt other people. It isn't nice.

Someone once defined maturity as not cheating on your partner.

You deserve better than this. Hold out for the gold ring - a ring of your very own.

PART TWO: Finding that Special Someone

How do you find that special someone? Stick with me kid, and I will show you the way.

In the olden days things were much simpler. There were arranged marriages and some of them actually worked out - so they tell me. However, this is the age of enlightenment and you are on your own!

If I may digress for a moment. If you haven't seen the film: *Crossing Delancy*, I would warmly recommend it. It is a delightful tale of a young, sophisticated, successful New Yorker whose grand-mother hires a professional matchmaker. It is a heart-warming story with a surprise ending. Go see it! You'll like it!

Back to the task at hand. How to meet someone. I will share with you my personal experiences and those of my friends, plus the fruits of much research gathered on the subject.

The following are some of the ways that you might consider meeting someone:

Family and friends

A time-honoured method. Next to matchmakers, this is the oldest way of going about it. It has a lot to recommend it. Your family and friends have your best interests at heart. They want you to be happy. They know you and they know the other person. If this is an option for you, don't dismiss it. You never know.

Your place of worship

Again, this one has a lot going for it. After all, you have a good spiritual base. You share some very important values. You probably know the person. Should the relationships evolve, you will have a solid foundation on which to build a future and your community will share in your happiness.

Follow your interests

Take a course, teach a course, learn a new language, travel, participate in sports, take up a hobby - do things that you enjoy and you will meet people who share your interests, your passions.

When doing things you are passionate about, it's like being a magnet for like-minded people. You are at your best, you are at ease, you love what you do and this makes you very attractive.

The rewards manifold: having the time of your life, meeting the kind of people who share your interests - one of whom might well become interested in you.

Volunteer

See above. For more on the subject, see chapter titled: SERVING YOUR COMMUNITY - VOLUNTEERING.

Dating Services

Try it and see what you think. In principle it seems like an excellent idea. You tell them the kind of person you are, the kind of person you want to meet and presto, you've got yourself a date. Probably better than a blind date or the bar scene.

As a matter of fact, I met my ex-husband through a computer dating service. I don't think that it is the system's fault necessarily that we got divorced! After all, we did stay married for 12 years and most of those were good years.

PART THREE: My Adventures in the "Personals"

"*Personals*" can be fun. For example, in addition to actually meeting people who became friends and lovers, I have also collected enough amusing anecdotes to dine out on for a long time to come.

The following ad appeared a number of times in some of the local newspapers and magazines. I know, because I put it there.

" *Mensch*" Wanted"*

You are: 40+, non-smoker, MENSA-calibre, romantic, emotionally mature, secure, funny, articulate, urban/e, classy, considerate, tender.

You like: old movies, Broadway, The Sunday New York Times, big bands, slow dancing, reading, walking and stimulating conversation.

As a result of this brazen action, I have met some interesting people and had some funny experiences.

I would like to share some of these experiences as a public service so that the people out there in the Wonderland of Personals might take heart in the knowledge that they are not alone.

---

* For the Yiddishly-challenged, a "*mensch*" is a considerate, kind, humane, good-hearted soul. An all-around good person. A prince among men. Now you see why I used "mensch."

One of the most puzzling aspects of this journey has been to hear from people who obviously did not read the ad. My guess would be that they answered every ad. I found this very strange because it costs time, energy and money to respond. Also some battering of the ego when they are rejected. Very odd, me thinks.

My ad stated "40+"; nevertheless, I heard from people in their 20's and 30's. One of these men told me that, in spite of his age, (late 20's), we had a lot in common. We both liked old movies. Upon further exploration, it became clear that our definition of "old movies" was somewhat different. His idea of an "old movie" was one that has been out for more than a year and is available on video. I didn't think we had as much in common as he did!

Then there was the gentleman farmer who felt that, once I experienced country life, I would love it as much as he did. This was in direct opposition to all my urban values. No matter. He felt confident that we had a good basis for a relationship. I demurred.

I also heard from a sports enthusiast who did not read my ad very carefully, if at all. There was not one word about sports. He suggested that we would enjoy watching the blue jays together. When I replied that I was not much of a bird-watcher, he said he liked my sense of humour! Who was joking? I had no idea who the blue jays were. (In all fairness to me, this was some years ago. I now know that the Blue Jays are a sports team.) After this encounter, one of my dear friends suggested that when I meet a sports-minded man, all

I need to say is: "How about those Blue Jays!" and then sit back and listen. The downside is that I have yet to find a sports enthusiast who also shares my love of the theatre, old movies and *The Sunday Times.*

One of my favourites was the gentleman who, although he did not know what "mensch", MENSA-calibre or urban/e meant, he was sure that he possessed those qualities. I was tempted to say: "If you don't know it - you ain't", but good manners and a kind heart prevented me from saying so.

Another gentleman responding to my ad assured me that he was a "mensch." We had a lovely chat and discovered that we had a lot in common. We met for coffee. I listened to him for an hour and fifteen minutes while he ranted and raved against everything under the sun. Finally, I excused myself to go to the washroom and to consider some graceful exit line. On my return I was shocked to find that he had left, leaving my coat and purse unattended in a busy restaurant. By me, he was no *"mensch!"*

And then there was the movie buff who assured me that he shared my love of old movies. As a matter of fact, he said, he will never forget those immortal last words from that great classic, *"Casablanca":* "Frankly my dear, I don't give a damn!" - and, strangely enough, neither did I!

I also spoke with a theatre aficionado who shared my love of the stage. He was pretty sure that he had seen something or other at the O'Keefe Centre not more than two or three years ago and he was planning to go again some time. Not with me, bub!

One of my strangest experiences was a dinner date with some unexpected twists. We had a nice long chat on the phone. He told me that he was a lawyer and financial advisor. He lived in a respectable part of the city, went to good schools and we knew some of the same people.

As it turned out, in addition to being a lawyer, he was a also a mercenary soldier, waiting to be called up at any moment. His hobbies included conspiracy theories and martial arts. He talked about "taking people out." He wore a shirt open to his navel. He had enough gold chains to start his own jewellery store and to make Mr.T. jealous. I fervently hope that he is not reading this book. He knows where I live!

And then there was the prominent psychiatrist. He never stopped being the professional that he was. All through dinner he analyzed everything I said and suggested that I needed intensive psycho-therapy. He, on the other hand, had everything under control in his own life. This included *paying* his children to spend time with him because he understood that money was their motivating force.

At the end of the evening he suggested that we play "kissy-face." This is a man in his fifties and English is his first language! One would think that he could do better than "kissy-face!" Not a match made in heaven. And no, we didn't play "kissy-face..."

I once went out with a charming man. We had a wonderful time. Talked till the wee hours of the morning and arranged to meet for lunch the next day. He never showed and the phone number that he gave me was out of service. Go figure!

In closing, let me say that I also met some fine people through the PERSONALS - some of whom became friends and lovers. It is for this reason that I keep on answering and placing these ads. I know that he is out there and someday I will find him. After all, *I only need one!*

Find yourself someone to love!

Suggestions for your search for a mate:

★ Find out who you are and what you need in a relationship

★ Explore avenues you have not tried before

★ Don't lose hope - remember:
   you only need one!

Money Matters

Let me start by saying that I like money - money is good and, like everything else in this book, these are personal views, views I have arrived at based on my experiences. As Mae West and Sophie Tucker said very wisely, *"I've been rich and I've been poor and rich is better."* Amen to that!

Yes, it is better to be rich than poor. However, after some basic needs are met - shelter, food, health, personal safety - how much *more* do you need? How important is money, really? More to the point, how important is it to have millions? What are you prepared to do for money? These are some of the questions that I would suggest you might pose to yourself.

Money and happiness

Having money does not automatically grant you happiness. A nicer car, a bigger house, a more lavish vacation, more CD's -yes money will buy you all of these. And it is nice to have these things. But, is it worth working around the clock 6 or 7 days a week? Not seeing your family or friends? I would suggest not. But don't take my word for it. You be the judge.

If you could buy happiness with money then the happiest people today would be the Royal family, the Kennedys, the Rothschilds, the Rockefellers, rock stars, sports stars - to name just a few. Unless you have been living on a desert island *(and if so, how did you get this book?)*, you know that many of these folks are not exactly living in happiness galore. Addictions, divorces, suicides, murders, fatal accidents, nasty court cases are just some of the issues they frequently face. None of these folks would qualify as poster boys/girls for the *"HAPPINESS IS..."* campaign.

Please understand, I am not suggesting that the rich are unhappy and the poor are happy. Of course not. I would just ask you to take a look at your own situation and consider where you stand on the issue. You may be surprised. Or maybe not. But it might be worth thinking about.

What money will NOT do

Consider this: the people who changed the history of the world were not the people with the most money. Think of some like: Lincoln, Marx & Engels, Einstein, Freud, Dr. Schweitzer, Stalin, Churchill, Gandhi, Mother Teresa - not a millionaire among them!

If changing the world is not your priority today, think about this: money does not solve life's big problems or the real issues that you face every day. It does not help if you are sick. Money cannot buy health or bring a loved one back to life. It won't help with your teenager, spouse or boss.

Money didn't save the six million Jews who perished during the holocaust or the other millions who have died and are still dying all over the world in war-torn areas.

It won't buy love or friendship, not the lasting kind, anyway. Temporary, maybe. When your money is gone, so is your money-bought lover or friend.

If money is your guiding value, you might consider what you are giving up and what you are getting. Very few people will say on their deathbed: *"Gee, I wish I spent more time at the office!"* Think about what's the use of working around the clock 7 days a week? When are you going to enjoy the fruits of your labour? When you are too old? Maybe your widow will be able to sow her wild oats when you're gone. Cheery thought, that!

When you work around the clock you are missing the important things in life, like being with your family. You miss watching your children grow up, their first step, school play, hockey games, their first date - a long list of missed opportunities that will never come back. Once your kids are grown, you won't see much of them. If you didn't build the familial bonds when they were growing up, it will be much harder, if not impossible, to re-establish them later.

Remember: *You can always make money later, but you cannot be a parent to a child later.* Is having a big bank account a consolation?

If making money is your first priority, then your mate, your family and friends will be shortchanged.

And, in the final analysis, you must ask yourself, is it really worth it?

To me, one of the saddest ideas of our time is that *he who dies with the most toys wins!* Am I the only one who thinks this is insane?

My idea of the perfect way to leave this world would be to check out when my checking account is empty, or even better, when I'm overdrawn! (Even the most committed of bank managers won't follow me to the other side, me thinks!) It makes sense to make and spend your money in this lifetime. Except for Shirley McLaine, the rest of us are not so sure about other lives.

Money - part of your value system

Your attitudes toward money, like other core values, are formed in early childhood. If you had a financially difficult childhood, it will colour your views till the end of your days. If you lived through the depression, that will also have an influence on your view unless some drastic event reshapes your values or you take steps to do so.

I'm sure you know people who are made of money and yet won't spend it. Some people still have the first dollar they ever made. They could have more money than King Midas and it would not improve their lives or make them happier.

Some years ago there was an economist who suggested that if all the money in the world were to be placed in one big pile and distributed evenly to everyone on earth, within one year we would all be back where we started.

Lottery winners are a example of this. There was a documentary on ABC television that touched upon how winning millions of dollars affect people's lives. The bottom line was that within one year most of the winners were back to where they were prior to winning. Not only that, but there were some serious downsides to their stories - loss of jobs, divorces and family feuds.

Of course, there were some winners who are perfectly happy and things are working out fine for them and their families. However, this show and other studies point to the same conclusion: winning the money will not change who you are - the leopard does not change his spots.

Chances are, you will not become a happy, benevolent, kind, generous and caring person over-night because you won some big bucks. You probably won't abolish world hunger, stop the arms race, find the cure for cancer or even the common cold.

The Hungarians

In addition to reading numerous studies about attitudes towards money, I was also able to observe an interesting phenomenon first-hand. I came to Canada in 1957, during the Hungarian revolution. There were many Hungarians who, like my family, settled in Montreal. It was amazing to watch their rise. Within about 10 years, most were at about the same or a higher living standard as the one they had back home.

I'll grant you that I don't have a statistically acceptable sample, nor do I have a control group. But, consider some of the obstacles: a new country, didn't speak the language, had no money, no connections, middle-aged, families to support - to name just a few. And, yet, within a short time, they overcame these obstacles and ended up as good or better than where they left off in Hungary a decade earlier.

Their progress paralleled what studies of other immigrants have shown: what you think and how you make money has more to do with your early childhood than external circumstances.

What money CAN do

When we got married I was under the impression that the division of labour between my husband and I was that he *made* the money and *I spent it!* And for the twelve years of our married life, I held up my end very well! And he did an excellent job at his end, too.

Our divorce was fairly simple and amicable, in part, because we had no large bank accounts, properties or investment portfolios to fight over. Due to my diligence in spending everything he earned, we had none of these!

Having money allows you many freedoms. Although not millionaires, we were comfortable. We didn't have to worry about the basics - putting a roof over our heads, feeding and clothing ourselves. Over and above that, we were able entertain, travel, go to the theatre, dine out, buy books and records (remember, these were the '70's!) -money allows you to do all this.

I was also able to indulge in two of my favourite pastimes: donating to worthy causes and buying presents. Speaking of presents, this was one of the areas where my husband and I had some problems. I operated under the assumption that since he loved me, he could read my mind and buy me the gifts that I wanted without me telling him.

When we first got married, I *hinted* that I *loved* Christmas music. For our first Christmas together he bought me Handel's *Messiah*. Second Christmas it was the Viennese Boys Choir singing traditional Christmas hymns. It wasn't until our third year together that I told him that for me Christmas music was Perry Como, Bing Crosby and Rosemary Clooney. The poor man didn't know - how could he?

Money also allowed me to write and publish this book. Since this is my first effort, there were no large (or small!) advance cheques to see me through the writing process. You need time to write. You also have to eat and have a roof over your head while you are writing - all of which takes money.

Mind you, my lifestyle is not one that would be profiled by Martha Stewart, but it did allow me to finish this book. For example, I live in a non-profit government co-op. I haven't had a vacation in more than 15 years. I am not able to make donations to worthy causes - although I do give my time and energy! I don't have a car. I don't drink or smoke. I am vegetarian, I buy day-old bread and the cheapest fruits and vegetables. My clothes are hand-me-downs from friends or from Goodwill. My books come from the library. But, at the end of the day, it is my choice. And, when (please note, I didn't say: *if!*) this book becomes a best seller and I make millions of dollars, I'll probably take a vacation, make large donations to my favourite causes, buy fresh bread and any fruits and vegetables that I like. I might even up-grade my clothes shopping from Goodwill to Value Village!

Make a budget - what a capital idea!

One way to manage your finances is to have a budget. You won't necessarily spend less money, but you will know where the money goes. And in an emergency it will be a big advantage because you will know where you can cut back. Also, you might consider living *below* your means and the budget will be an essential tool. I know that living below your means is an unusual idea, but some people, including me, are promoting it.

In the early years of our marriage we had a budget. It was a formal affair. My husband was an engineer and he knew about rules. We had a written budget and little brown envelopes for each category. At the first of each month, we would sit down at the kitchen table and sort the money into the envelopes. The system worked fine until one day, the 20th of the month to be exact, when the little brown envelope marked "food" was empty. Nothing, nil, zip, nada.

My husband, who was otherwise a very sensible and clever chap, said in all seriousness: "Well, that's it. We won't eat until the next pay cheque." I did point out, without much success, that we did have money in some of the other little brown envelopes. My husband was adamant: no money, no food. After some discussion, he did come around and we did dip into some of the other little brown envelopes.

I would recommend a budget (a little less strict, of course!), whether you are single, married, divorced, starting out or retired. It might not change your spending habits but it will certainly be a sobering and educational experience. If you have children who are old enough, by all means, include them in the exercise. It will give them an idea where their allowance comes from.

Also encourage them to have their own bank account. I say this in spite of what my grown daughter tells me was one of her more dramatic experiences when she was growing up.

Apparently (and I am taking her word for this, because I don't remember), I insisted that she open a bank account. What she remembers is that she gave her money to the bank and I told her that the bank will give it to other people! As far as she was concerned, I was crazy, but I was bigger and she felt she had better go along with this loony idea. In my defense, I must say that I probably explained the part about the bank lending money to other people and paying interest, but either she forgot or I did not explain it to her all that well!

Her other early contact with money was somewhat less dramatic. When she was about 3 or 4 years old, a friend of ours gave her a ten dollar bill. She very graciously said: "Thank you very much for the dime." Well, at least she got the digits right!

Being creative with your money

Consider ways of being creative with your money. For example, one of my great passions is the theatre. Over the past number of years I have not been able to support the arts as much as I would have liked. So, I came up with the following idea: I would hire students from the theatre school for odd jobs around the house. I was able to pay them and they got the jobs done. Instead of donating money, which I couldn't afford, I hired them. It worked out well.

When I moved, I hired a whole gang of theatre school students to help. In the last seven years I have moved twice and both times I hired a crew from the theatre school and have been very happy with the results.

As a matter of fact, for one of the moves, I wasn't even in town. They packed my stuff, hired a van and unpacked at the new place. One of the added bonuses both for myself and the crew was that I was moving to a smaller place and whatever did not fit, I donated to the moving crew!

The point is that I was making a contribution to the future of Canadian theatre. The crew got paid, had pizza and beer and also received some furniture. All in all, not a bad deal.

Think about how *you* can be creative with your money. Keep in mind that you can't take it with you. (Although, I had a friend who said, if he can't take it with him, he is not going. And to his credit, he did not go until he was in his late 90's. But, alas, he did not take it with him.)

And, even when things are tight, consider giving a percentage to charity. It will make you feel better, I guarantee it.

Live long & prosper!

Some ideas ideas for you to consider:

★ Try living within your means: if you don't have it, don't spend it

★ Try living *below* your means - yes, it is possible and it is *not* against the law!

★ *Leave home without* your American Express/Visa/Mastercard

★ Make a budget and stick to it. There are many excellent books on the subject available at banks and libraries

★ Pay yourself first - save 10% of your income

★ Check out money-saving ideas in your local newspapers or get some books from the library

★ Give regularly to charity

★ Consider leaving a percentage of your estate in your will to worthy organizations

Serving Your Community: Volunteering

"You make a living from what you get, but you make a life from what you give." - Winston Churchill

Volunteering is the best thing you can do for yourself and your community. It isn't often that you can do something for others that can't help but benefit you. Very often your rewards will outweigh your efforts. I can tell you from personal experience that volunteering has enriched my life beyond measure.

One of my current volunteer efforts is at a church where we serve a vegetarian meal to anyone who wishes to join us. There is no preaching, no guilt trips, just a hot meal with no strings. The tables are set with care. The service is with a smile. The food is wholesome and plentiful. At the end of the meal the guests are encouraged to take food home. We provide containers and shopping bags.

It is a humbling and spiritually up-lifting experience. It is never far from my mind that there but for the grace of God go I. Of course, it would be wonderful if we didn't have to have soup kitchens, but the reality is that we serve 200-300 people every week. Ours is just one of many such programs. If you are able to volunteer, thank your lucky stars that you are on the giving end. Things could change, and you may end up on the receiving end.

Benefits - Why you "should" volunteer

One of the many great benefits of volunteering is the opportunity to learn new skills. This is your chance to learn how to run a meeting, how to be an effective and productive member of a team, develop artistic talents, public speaking skills, accounting, marketing - to name just a few.

Especially in today's tight economic conditions, it is always useful to learn new skills. Even better if it is not costing you money, and you are doing good at the same time. A win/win situation all around.

The other great benefit is that volunteer jobs often turn into paying positions. After all, if there is a vacancy, you will know about it. The people who run the place are familiar with you. They don't have to go to the expense of advertising. You are there and you already know the ropes. You're a shoe-in.

Volunteering looks good on a resume. Whether you are starting out and have no experience or thinking of changing fields, having been a volunteer will give you a leg up. You know from your own experience that if you are looking to hire someone, and, other considerations being equal, someone who has given back to the community will have an edge in getting the position. Sometimes, nice guys do finish first!

Volunteering broadens your horizon. You learn new things. You get out of your rut. You are contributing to the common good. You will discover new talents, abilities you didn't know you had. This is your chance to try new things.

You make a difference. This is what it's all about. Improving the world. Leaving the planet a better place for having lived here.

You meet the nicest people when you volunteer. (Nasty folks don't!) These are the people who share your view of the world. People who make a difference. People who believe they are their brothers' keepers, who believe in giving back to their community.

You will also meet the most interesting people. They lead interesting lives and participate in worthwhile activities. You will want to be around these people because they will make you feel good about yourself.

It is energizing to be with people who share your passion. Usually there is very little or no politics/ power plays. You are there to do a good job for a cause that you all believe in. This is all for the good.

You can find out what other exciting things your fellow volunteers are involved in and you might find other worthy causes. You can also meet business contacts, make friends and find lovers.

An opera-lover friend of mine used to be an extra on the stage. You know, carrying spears and that sort of thing. He met his wife, who was also one of the extras, at the Metropolitan Opera in New York. They have been happily married for over 30 years.

Then there are other perks too. Another opera-lover friend, who, as a volunteer, gets to meet the performers, see dress rehearsals and attends social functions with other volunteers and the cast. One of her recent volunteer jobs was being personal chauffeur for one of the out-of-town stars. She picked him up at the airport, took him to his hotel. And, in return for her efforts she got a ticket to opening night and to the party afterwards. I'd say she got a good deal.

One of the scariest thoughts that I sometimes consider is what would happen if volunteers were to stop volunteering. It is something to think about. In these difficult financial times, the government would not step in to fill the vacuum and the people who can least afford it would suffer.

Where to volunteer

Find causes that you believe in. If you are having problems deciding, check out your local Volunteer Bureau or your newspapers. Here are some suggest-ions you might consider:
- religious/spiritual groups
- arts and culture
- political organizations
- health organizations

- women's/men's groups
- social agencies
- service groups
- educational
- neighbourhood clubs
- Big Brothers/Big Sisters

The list is truly endless. Anything that you can support whole-heartedly is the ideal place for you to be. After all, you are volunteering your time and expertise, so you might as well pick something that you are passionate about and have fun doing.
My personal motto is: *"If it ain't fun, I ain't doin' it!"* So, have fun!

Personal experiences

One of the side benefits that I have personally experienced over the years is that volunteering enabled me to go places that I could not otherwise afford. Since I have more time than money, I will call an organization that is putting on an event I would like to attend and say: "I would very much like to come to your event but, unfortunately, I can't afford to buy a ticket. Do you need any volunteers?" You can offer to take tickets, serve coffee, paint the scenery, set up, clean up - whatever talents you have, someone can use them.

You would be surprised at the number of events I have attended over the years. I have no problem calling any organization because I am a great believer in what goes around, comes around. I do good for the community and the community acknowledges my efforts. Often I get calls from people offering me free tickets because they know that I do a lot of volunteer work.

There is no shame in admitting that you are temporarily at a low ebb in you financial situation. Your offer of help will benefit both parties. You will be able to attend some functions that you couldn't afford and the organization is reaping the benefit in many ways. They are getting help that they would otherwise have to pay for. They have an enthusiastic person who supports their cause and that enthusiasm will make their event even more enjoyable for the people you come in contact with.

Remember: *you cannot hire enthusiasm!*

Over the years I have also volunteered to be part of medical research projects pertaining to cholesterol and asthma - issues which affect me personally.

If you have the opportunity to volunteer for such projects, I would encourage you to do so because:

- for the duration of the study you will get the best medical care that money can buy because the research grants go to the top medical practitioners in the field
- you will undergo extensive testing and they may find early warning signs of other problems that you are not aware of (this happened to me)
- your medication is free, the most up-to-date and with the least amount of side effects
- your illness might improve because of the new medications (mine did)

- you are helping medical science (and, therefore, mankind) in finding new and more
effective cures

As an added bonus, in my cholesterol study, food was provided!

Talk to your doctor or call up a hospital or university to find out what research projects are currently looking for participants.

And, while we're on the subject of health and volunteering, please consider bone marrow registry, being a blood donor as well as an organ donor. Giving blood is easy and the life you save might be someone near and dear to you. Offering to become an organ donor (hopefully not in the near future!) is also very simple. Just indicate it on your driver's licence.

Politics is another area where I have had several decades of volunteer experience. Over the years I have worked on many campaigns across Canada. There are many benefits in working for a candidate. You are working with like-minded people who share your passion - always a good thing! This is your opportunity to participate in democracy. It is, in fact, your civic duty!

If your candidate wins, there is a wonderful victory party and you now know your representative. If your candidate didn't win, there is always a next time. In the meantime, I would suggest that you get to know the winning candidate. She or he is your representative and part of a team that makes decisions that affect you - you want to know people like that!

Awakening Your Life Skills

Final thoughts: Service to your community is a major part of most religions. Even if you are not religious, being community-minded is an up-lifting experience. There are no down-sides to volunteering. It is non-toxic, non-fattening and it doesn't cost a dime. It is one of the best things you can do for yourself and your community.

Get out there and volunteer!

Suggested activities:

★ make a list of causes that you are passionate about, then call up and volunteer

★ if you don't know where to start, talk to your family, friends, co-workers, check out your local volunteer centre and your library

Simplify! Simplify! Simplify!

*I*f there was one thing that I would wish to convince you to do, it would be to simplify your life. If you need an incentive to do this, consider the possibility of *being forced to do so* because of circumstances beyond your control. You might get downsized, you might get sick. I don't like being the bearer of bad news - remember, for me the glass is always half full! However, the reality is that a lot of us will be facing one or both of these possibilities.

So, consider this a dry run. At least you will know that you *can* manage, if need be. It's a wonderfully empowering feeling just knowing that you *can*. And if, God forbid, the worst comes to pass, you will be in fine shape to face whatever comes. Being able to face whatever life throws at you is one of the hallmarks of a happy, well-balanced life.

Don't major in minor things...

...in other words, don't sweat the small stuff. Concentrate on the important things in life. Nurture your relationships with family and friends. Attend to your physical, mental and emotional well-being. Life is too short to worry about the small stuff. Don't let the tail wag the dog. You are here for a short time, make it count. Enjoy, enjoy, enjoy. It's your life and you are the one making decisions on how best to live it. *Life is for living.*

And, now for the bad news: *NO ONE GETS OUT ALIVE!* If you've seen the movie *"Garbo Speaks"* you might recall the scene where Anne Bancroft, on being told that she was dying, was very surprised. When her son tells her that we all have to die sometime, she replies: "Yes, I know, but I thought I might be the exception."

The good news is that you are alive *NOW.* I am assuming that you are alive, since you are reading this book. On the other hand...if you are reading it in some other dimension, would you please call me *immediately!* I would love to hear from you.

But seriously folks, while you are alive, the sky is the limit. You can and should do whatever your heart desires. Don't let the unimportant and the trivial sap your energy. Go for the gusto. You cannot do everything, but you can do some things. Life is like a big department store. *You can have anything you want, but you cannot have everything you want.* Where would you put it all, anyway? So go for the big stuff, the important stuff and don't let the small stuff get in the way.

Carpe Diem - seize the day

Your life would be much simpler if you lived it day by day. Today is all you have. As someone once said: "Yesterday is history, tomorrow is a mystery but today is a gift, that's why it's called the present." Enjoy today. Today is all you have, all any of us have. Live each day as if it were your last day. Be good to yourself and others. That's what we are here for, to do good. Help ourselves and our fellow human beings. Be good to the animals and to Mother Earth. As corny as it sounds, *what goes around comes around.* Some people call that "karma." You don't have to believe in reincarnation to behave in a principled way.

I once had an instructor who, when asked if she believed in reincarnation, replied: "I didn't believe in it in my past lives and I won't believe in it in my future lives!" And there you have it.

The bottom line is:
Today is all you have. Don't waste it.

A filing system for simplifying your life

Let me share with you a filing system that I find simple and easy. What you need is:
  - one accordion file numbered 1 - 31
  - 8 file folders marked:

THIS MONTH	BILLS
NEXT MONTH	TO DO
THIS YEAR	FOLLOW-UP
NEXT YEAR	FILE

The secret of efficiency is this: *handle each piece of paper only once.*

As I open my mail:

1. I attend to what needs immediate attention
2. Remaining items get slotted into the appropriate folders
3. At the first of each month I:
   a) pay the bills
   b) do the filing
   c) take NEXT MONTH's folder and sort what's in there into the accordion file

Every morning I look into that day's slot and there I have everything I need. It is simple, easy and it works. You are welcome to use it.

Simplifying your communication

I have found the following ideas to be useful in simplifying both business and personal communications.

1. PAST/PRESENT/FUTURE
   Using this format as your framework will help you organize your thoughts. It will give a logical and easy-to-follow flow to your ideas.
   For example, a thank you note might read as follows:

   "Thank you very much for the lovely week-end at your cottage. We enjoyed our stay with you.

   We think of you every time we eat one of those delicious tomatoes from your garden.

   We look forward to seeing you soon."

2. WHO/WHAT/WHERE/WHEN/WHY
   Like the Past/Present/Future format, this will also
   help you to organize your thoughts. I use this
   format for many things. For example, it works
   really well for party invitations.

Simplify! Simplify! Simplify!

***Some other ideas you might consider
for simplifying your life:***

★ don't keep up with the Joneses

★ get rid of clothes you haven't worn in the
  past year

★ walk instead of driving

Stress Management

After ten years of researching stress, here is what I came up with:

In order to reduce stress in your life:

1. DO MORE OF WHAT YOU LIKE TO DO
2. DO LESS OF WHAT YOU DON'T LIKE TO DO

Let me repeat this: *to reduce stress in your life:*

1. DO MORE OF WHAT YOU LIKE TO DO
2. DO LESS OF WHAT YOU DON'T LIKE TO DO.

That's it folks! This is the secret of stress management. However, it has not had the attention it deserves because there is no money to be made from this idea!

What I propose is simple but not easy. First you *have to* identify what you like and what you don't like. Now obviously, you cannot always do what you would like and you cannot avoid doing some things that are not your favourite. What I would like to suggest is that once you have identified your likes and dislikes, concentrate on what brings you joy.

I know that life is not always fair. You can't always do what you want. But, you would be amazed at how much you *can do* once you have identified and *have given yourself permission* to do what pleases you.

Remember *The "Not So" Stern Rules*, my litmus test for doing something. If you are in doubt, ask yourself the three questions:

1. Is it against the law?
2. Will anyone, including you, get hurt?
3. Are you able and willing to deal with the consequences?

If you can answer NO to questions 1 and 2, and YES to question 3, go ahead and do it. It is your life. Go for it!

Go with the flow

Stress management experts talk about the "fight or flight" response. This goes back to our early history as a species when faced with a lion, you either fought or took flight - depending on how hungry you were!

Unfortunately, these responses are hard-wired into our brain. Not too many of us face the lion, but we respond the same way to an angry boss or unhappy spouse. Let me suggest another way. When you are faced with a stressful situation, consider a third alternative: don't react immediately, give yourself a chance to consider your options. Stall for time.

While you have no control over your boss' anger or your spouse's unhappiness, you do have control over your reaction. You always have options. You can choose to react in any number of ways.

For example, if your boss is on a tirade about something, let him go on with it. Don't interrupt. Eventually he will run out of steam. After all, how long can one go on? While he is ranting and raving and getting himself all worked up, you stay calm, listen, and consider your options. When he is finished, you can calmly state your reaction. As a general rule, the more the other person raises his voice, the more you should lower yours.

Going with the flow saves so much energy. Remember: *It is always easier to ride the horse in the direction that it is going!* If you have ever seen or done any martial arts, you will know that when your opponent strikes, you don't strike back, you go with the flow and pull back. You let your opponent's energy dissipate.

Everyone has stress

Just in case you are ready to feel sorry for yourself for all the stress in your life, keep in mind that we all have stress in our lives. No one is exempt. Stress is no respecter of age, colour, religion, social status, money or power.

Sometimes, the grass seems greener on the other side. Before you envy your neighbours, remember two things. First, you don't really know what their stresses are. Second, there is an old Russian folk tale about how, if everybody in the world put their worries into a bag and put all the bags together in one big pile, we would all choose our own bag of troubles.

Like most things in life, how you deal with stress is in part genetic. If you are born with "worry" genes, it's like having blue eyes and blond hair - it goes with the territory. However, genetics is only one part of the equation and there are many other factors that come into play.

Mark Twain said that he had lots of worries in his lifetime, most of which never materialized. Live in the moment. After all, this is all you have. Yesterday is gone and it ain't never coming back. Tomorrow may never come. But today, ah, today: this is it, this is your moment in the sun, enjoy it, make the most of it. Like I said, "Carpe diem" - seize the day. Live each day as if it were your last - because it might well be!

Identify your stressors

Your stressors are your own. What stresses one person out, gives another person joy. For example, there was a study done recently that indicated that most people in the United States were scared to death of speaking in public. As I was reading the results, I was amazed. I love to speak in public. It gives me joy. Not only does it not stress me out, it energizes me. So there you have it. Different strokes for different folks.

Make a list of things that stress you. Look at it carefully. Your list will likely fall into the following four categories: work, money, health and relationships. Identify and deal with the issues.

It's not much use for you to say: "my boss stresses me out, my kids, my wife, my friends, the other drivers...etc etc". Let's be honest: there aren't too many people in your life who get up and start the day by saying: "Today I will make Joe/Jane's life miserable. I will increase his/her stress level a hundred-fold." The bottom line is: *what stresses you out are not the actions of the people in your life, it is your reaction to those actions.*

For example, one of my biggest personal stressors is when I'm talking to people on the phone and they take another call. I know it is called call-waiting, but I call it call-rude. The idea, of course, is to check if the other caller is more important or more interesting. My solution is to tell my friends that I will not hold on when they take another call. They are free to call me back later. Of course, this doesn't work in all situations, but you would be amazed how often it does.

Look at your stressors. They will fall into two basic categories: one that is within your control and one that is outside of your control. It is a sobering exercise. Unless you are a dictator, you are only in control of yourself, your actions and your reactions. (Sad, but true.)

Oh, I know we have illusions of control over children, employees, friends, students - but that is all they are: illusions. You may indeed have temporary control over your children, but ultimately, they will be their own masters. (And a recent study indicates that peer influence is stronger than parental influence.) Your employees - again, yes you have temporary control, but in the long run, they are their own masters. Ditto for spouses and students and anybody else.

You *have control* over losing weight, stoping smoking or not taking drugs. You *have no control* over your spouse or children doing these things. You *have control* over whether to buy gold or not. You *have no control* over the price of gold. Just a bit of reality check, folks!

If you have problems separating what's within your control and what is not, you might, again, recite *The Serenity Prayer:*

> *"God grant me the SERENITY to accept the things I cannot change, COURAGE to change the things I can and the WISDOM to know the difference."*

You might also recall the Buddhist saying on worrying:

> *"There is no reason to worry.*
> *If you can solve your problem,*
> *then why worry.*
> *If you cannot,*
> *then what's the use of worrying."*

And there you have it in a nut shell.

I am not always able to follow my own good advice, or course. Being human, at times I fall into the *"do as I say, not as I do"* trap.

In the early 80's I had a bookstore. When it first opened I had visions of people breaking down the door to buy my wonderful selection of books. Well, it didn't quite work out that way. Things were slow at the beginning and I was stressed out. Fortunately, I had a wise partner who said to me: "It will take time. Have patience. Remember when you were pregnant?

It takes nine months (give or take) no matter what you do. You can drink milk till the cows come home, you can exercise for hours daily and you can visualize and meditate for all your worth; the baby still will not come any earlier. So it is with the store. It takes what it takes." Wise words.

So, this is my advice to you: keep in mind the Serenity Prayer, the Buddhist saying and my wise friend's remark: things take what time they take and you being stressed out over it will not make it happen any sooner. In fact, it may delay things. So, take it easy and try to relax. You might as well.

Saying "NO"

One of the hardest and most stressful things for most of us is saying NO to loved ones, friends, neighbours, co-workers. Most of us would like to be good guys and go along with people we care about. Alas, you cannot please all the people all the time. And it really is OK to say NO. Sometimes that is all you can and should say, to reduce your stress.

Again, what I am talking about here is being reasonable and fair. One of the biggest stressors people put on themselves is taking on too many tasks because they cannot say no. Well, folks, sometimes you just have to bite the bullet and face the consequences.

People don't like to say no for a number of reasons. Sometimes you might feel that you are "letting down your side." Sometimes it is a control issue. Other times it might be fear, fear that if you say no, people might be able to get along without your help! Or it might be a loss of power. And it can be a feeling that if you say no, the other person will fall apart. Well, I am here to tell you that you would be surprised at how rarely people will fall apart because you say "no" to them! In my experience, practically never.

Let me repeat, *it is OK to say NO at times.* And you don't even have to explain or make up excuses. For example, the idea of you baking cookies, after a hard day's work, at midnight for your daughter's school bake sale is not the best use of your time or energy! For heaven's sake, go to your friendly neighbourhood bakery and buy the cookies. I can guarantee you that the kids won't know the difference, nor do they care. As a matter of fact they might even prefer store-bought to home-made.

Another way of lessening your stress is not to take on other people's stresses. This is really a way of saying NO. *It is OK* to say to someone: "I know that you would like me to take this off your shoulder, but I really can't. I'm sorry. It is really your problem and you will have to deal with it." Again, they will not crumble to pieces or exile you from their lives because you said no. And, if they do, you must ask yourself how solid or positive was this relationship anyway?

Relaxation

One of the most effective and most widely used ways of lowering stress is relaxation. While relaxation may mean many different things to each of us, (some people find sky diving relaxing!) breathing slowly and deeply is the easiest and cheapest, and everyone can benefit from it. Yes, I know, we all breathe, but have you given any thought to the importance of breathing? Consider this: you can go without food and water for a long time, but without air in your system you die.

Having had numerous asthma attacks, I can tell you that it is truly terrifying, one of scariest experiences anyone can have. In many other medical emergency situations you know that, no matter how much pain you are suffering, once the paramedics arrive they will relieve your pain. On the other hand, with an asthma attack the reality is that if you don't get air into your system within minutes, you die.

You don't have to be an asthmatic to realize the importance of breathing. Common sense will tell you that. I would like to encourage you to breathe deeply and slowly. If possible, breathe "good" air. What is good air? If you can, spend time outdoors, be with nature as much as you can. Indoors: use air purifiers, either man-made or, better yet, natural ones: plants.

In some cultures it is believed that when you are born you are given so many breaths. When you have used up your allotted number, your life ends. The slower you breathe, the longer you will live. Whether you subscribe to this belief or not, the bottom line is that slow, deep breathing is good for you.

When you are stressed, your breathing is shallow and rushed. Just by breathing more slowly and more deeply you reduce your stress. By taking three or four deep breaths you will feel better. (There are many excellent books on the subject. Many of the oriental disciplines such as yoga, qi kung and tai chi have breathing incorporated into the positions. Check them out.)

> *A simple breathing exercise is to breathe in, hold your breath and breathe out to the count of 4-6-8. Breathe in for the count of four, hold for count of six and breathe out to the count of eight.*
>
> *Do three to five of this in the morning and at night and you will notice a difference in your stress level.*

When I first came to Canada, I remember there was a Hungarian doctor whose English was less than perfect. He would tell his patients to: "INSPIRE and EXPIRE." Well, he knew what he meant, and presumably so did his patients, since none of them "EXPIRED" on his command. And, you know, he wasn't that far off. Inspiration could be close to breathing. (A friend of mine's son used to say: "inhale" and "outhale" - makes sense to me!)

In some languages the same word is used for "breath" and "spirit." In Latin: *spiritus*, in Hebrew: *ruach*, in Greek: *pneuma* and in Sanskrit: *prana*.

Physical

One of the greatest stress relievers is sex (with or without a partner!), so do it as often as you can.

Any kind of physical activity that you enjoy will help you reduce your stress.

Meditation

For some people the word "meditation" conjures up images of yogis sitting in lotus position on a mountain top in Nepal. And, certainly, that is one way of doing it, but there are many others. Let me hasten to add, I do not wish to discourage anyone from going to Nepal and sitting in a lotus position and meditating. Far from it. If you can, by all means go for it!

If, on the other hand, your budget doesn't allow for the trip, you can still meditate in your own living room or den or any other comfortable place.

I would like to dispel some of the myths around meditation: *you don't have to sit in the lotus position or subscribe to some weird eastern religion.* Neither of these is a prerequisite for meditation. Nor do you have to give your life's savings or your first-born to some Indian guru to give you a "mantra" and teach you meditation skills.

Just remember that meditation was brought to the West from the East. Its practitioners, who became the teachers for us Western folks, were in most cases Indians from India. For them, sitting in lotus position for hours was simple; they were comfortable doing it. They were also brought up in the religion.

On the other hand, we Western folk are *not* comfortable in the lotus position and sitting in that position for any length of time is a pain for most of us. Therefore, it would defeat the purpose.

You need not follow Hinduism or Buddhism to meditate. You can meditate by focusing on your breath. And you can make up your own "mantra".

To begin with, make sure that you will not be disturbed. Sit comfortably. You can close your eyes or not, as you prefer.

I find that closing my eyes works for me, but it is your choice.

If you want to meditate on your breath, just follow the air as it comes and goes. Notice which nostril you are breathing with. You only breathe through one nostril at a time. Just pay attention to the air coming in and going out. If your mind wonders, just bring it back to your breathing. If you have some thoughts crossing your mind, think of them as clouds in the sky. Acknowledge them and then let them pass out of your consciousness.

If you want to meditate on a word, your "mantra", pick something that has meaning for you. If you are of a spiritual nature, pick one from your religion. For example, sometimes I use "Shalom" as my mantra. But you can use any word that is meaningful for you. You can change your mantra. Some ideas for you to consider: peace, love, health.

Or you might want to meditate on a phrase or a poem that is meaningful for you. There is a lovely Buddhist meditation that I like very much:

May I be well and happy and
free from suffering
May I be peaceful and free
from fear and conflict.

You can also meditate on a flower, a candle or a beautiful object. You can listen to your favourite music. In fact, my Zen master believes that anything that you do that you are totally absorbed in is a form of meditation. If you are peeling potatoes with total concentration on just that and nothing else, then you are meditating!

In addition to sitting meditation, you can also do moving meditations. My Zen master worked with teenagers who wanted to move and he encouraged them to work with their breath and body movements. For example, you can breathe in and raise your arms and breathe out and lower your arms.

There is also a well-know Buddhist walking meditation that is called either the *Monk's Walk* or the *Warrior's Walk* - depending on who your teacher was. You take one step as you breathe in and another step as you breathe out. It looks very majestic when you watch it. It is very simple and yet very powerful. If you can, find a natural setting.

You might want to time your meditation with the sunrise and the sunset. Or first thing when you get up and last thing before you go to bed. It works best if you can establish a routine.

What is important is that whatever you do has meaning for you and that you stay with it. Start with 5 - 10 minutes and increase it at your own comfort level. The suggested times are 20 - 45 minutes, once or twice a day. Do what you can. It's your life and you're in charge. Do what works for you. And, like everything else, *it works if you work it!*

Praying / Chanting / Visualization / Affirmation

For some people, *prayers* work. If you are so inclined, you might want to read a page or chapter from your religious text.

Others find *chanting* a wonderful way to relax and reduce stress. Most religions have chanting as their regular practices. If you are not comfortable doing it out loud on your own, you may want to start doing it silently. You might find that eventually you want to chant out loud. See what works for you.

Visualization is another effective form of stress management. If you would like to, just get comfortable, make sure you're not disturbed, close your eyes, take some deep breaths and start visualizing yourself being very, very relaxed. Try it, you might like it. If you would like to learn more about visualization, one of the more popular book on the subject is Shakti Gawain's *Creative Visualization*. But any book that grabs your attention will be fine.

Affirmations are another activity some people find useful in dealing with stress. As the word says, you *affirm* what you would like to see happen in your life. Remember to keep it positive. For example, you might say: *"I am calm and relaxed."* Repeat it as often you like. One of the more popular affirmations is the following:

Every day in every way I am getting better and better.

In closing, let me say that none of the above are magic bullets. Some work for some people some of the time. You are the best judge of how you can reduce your stress. You know what your stressors are and how best to deal with them.

Stress is in itself neither good or bad. It is your reaction to the stressors in your life that makes the difference. Your stress level is under your control to quite a degree. Remember, it is *your* life and *you are in control.*

"STRESSED" is "DESSERTS" spelled backwards!

Should the spirit move you,
you might consider:

★ Do more of what you like/less of what you don't like

★ Go with the flow

★ List your stressors and examine them

★ Say "NO" more often

★ Breathe deeply and slowly

★ Exercise

★ Meditate

★ Pray

★ Repeat THE SERENITY PRAYER

★ List your favourite stress reducers and do them often

Wrap-Up

*I*n closing, let me share with you what this past year has been like for me. Among other things: my mother passed away, I was sick for three months, lost half a year's income and couldn't find a publisher for this book.

But, I survived all of the above and lived to tell the tale. I reaffirmed my belief that *we are not given more than we can handle.*

I was also able to crystallize my ideas on how we can be of help to each other in our time of need. This is what I learned:

1. If you need help, you have to let people know - if you don't tell them, they can't help you
2. Be specific about the *kind* of help you need - your friends and family aren't mind-readers
3. Say "thank you" - when people go out of their way to be helpful, express your appreciation:
   by phone - good
   thank you note - better
   publicly - the best

Let me illustrate.

My mother's death

My mother's funeral was in another city. When I got home, I called friends and I also called my synagogue, Congregation Darchei Noam in Toronto, where I was a new member. I thought I would like to have some form of a memorial service.

My small studio apartment can only accommodate about ten people. I needed a bigger place. One of my fellow congregants offered her home. Someone else organized the food. Rabbi Pinsker, who although didn't know my mother, delivered a very touching memorial. He also helped me through some of the rough times. A lot of people were there for me with prayers and support when I needed them, for which I was grateful. I could not have done it without their help.

I wrote letters of thanks to the person who opened her home to us for the service, to the person who organized the food and, of course, to Rabbi Pinsker. I also thanked people publicly at the synagogue and in our newsletter.

The point is this: *I asked for support, I was specific about what I needed and I thanked the people who were there for me in my time of need.*

My illness

I was sick for three months. (Usually I am a very healthy person and have not had any serious illness in about 15 years. I got sick shortly after my mother's death, I guess my resistance was down.)

Part of that time I was too weak to get out bed. I did not eat for a week. Going to the washroom tired me out. I had no energy to turn on the TV. In other words, things were really bad. I got through it with the support of many people.

Again, I called on my fellow congregants. They prayed for me. They brought food and did the dishes. And once I was feeling better, came to visit and took me out for meals. The Rabbi and others called frequently to see how I was doing.

My friends and fellow co-op members did my grocery shopping, drove me to the doctor and went to the drugstore for me.

And again, I was pro-active. I told people that I needed help. I was very specific. For example, I wanted cooked food because I could not stand long enough to prepare anything. Later, I just wanted company. And, when I was feeling better, I invited these friends for a thank you luncheon. And, of course, everyone got a thank you note and a public acknowledgement.

After my mother's death and during my illness, I also got a lot of support from people who are my fellow volunteers. Another reason for volunteering.

The publication of this book

I started writing this book on an electric typewriter. In part, this was due to my being Luddite and also because I couldn't afford a computer. And then one of my fellow co-op members gave me one. (Thank you, Claudia.) When I told people that I now had a computer, they were pleased for me. Although when I mentioned that it was a *Commodore*, they laughed! Well, they also laughed at Christopher Columbus!

In any case, I finished the book, and I sent outlines and sample chapters to a number of publishers. None of them were interested in publishing it. As matter of fact, some of them didn't even bother replying. And then came my mother's death, my illness and I put the project on hold. After I recovered, I decided that if nobody wants to publish it, I would do it myself. I don't give up easily! And that is how you come to hold this book in your hand.

Closing thoughts

It has been a hellish year. But, I got through it with a lot of help from my friends, members of Congregation Darchei Noam, members of my co-op and fellow volunteers. And, after all is said and done, I am glad to be alive and *the glass is still half full!*

Thank you for sharing this journey with me. I hope you enjoyed reading it I as much as I enjoyed writing it.

In Appreciation

I would like to express my heart-felt appreciation to the people who helped me. While writing is a solitary task, it could not happen without the support of many people.

Thanks to: *Judy Brunsek* for the life-saving suggestions; *Elisabeth Ecker* for encouragement and support; *Shirley Garfinkel* for your warmth, wit, generousity of spirit, support and all around good fellowship; *Hal Johnson* for sharing your wisdom so generously; *Doug Kehoe* for all the years of friendship, generousity and fun; *Brian Kremen and Bob Missen*, my fellow *Musketeers* for all the good times and the heart-to-hearts; *Blanche Muskovitsch* for all those years of loving kindness and support; Rabbi *Larry Pinsker* for your insight, support and time - above and beyond the call of duty; *Kathleen Sharpe* for your sense of humour and wisdom; *Carl Stacy* for your expertise, humour, generousity and being there for me at my time of need.

It was my great good fortune to able to assemble a dream team for the professional support, a team that was there for me in so many ways. Appreciation and thanks to: *Fortunato Aglialoro* for the wonderful design, your great sense of humour and enthusiasm; *Lori Rennie* of Transcontinental Printing for being the consummate professional, helpful and more; *Eric Hellman* for insightful editing; *Bill Hushion* for selling the book and giving time and support beyond any reasonable expectations.

I could not have done it without you. Thank you, one and all.

Living Skills for the 21st Century

How to lead a less stressful, happier, more
productive & balanced life

⌒∞⌒

SEMINARS
LIFESTYLE COACHING
KEYNOTES

⌒∞⌒

A light-hearted, pragmatic and humorous look
at some skills and techniques to help you cope
with the stresses of day-to-day living.

Topics:

Alternative Practices, Diet & Nutrition,

Goal Setting, Happiness Is..., Laughter & Humour,

Lifestyle Choices, Meditation, Money Matters,

Relationships, Relaxation, Simplifying Your Life

Stress Management & Volunteering

Your presenter, **Susan Stern** is the host of the
popular television series:
***HEALTHY ALTERNATIVES - An Introduction
to Alternative Practices and Lifestyle Choices.***
She is an experienced speaker who brings a sense
of humour and '*joie de vivre*' to her topics.

⌒∞⌒

SUSAN STERN SEMINARS
(416) 489-4541